P9-DHQ-698

For Karol
and Dave
from Ed Laurie

The Devil's Own Imp

Edward J. Laurie

March 14, 2007

authorHOUSE®

AuthorHouse™
1663 Liberty Drive, Suite 200
Bloomington, IN 47403
www.authorhouse.com
Phone: 1-800-839-8640
This book is a work of non-fiction. Unless otherwise noted, the author
and the publisher make no explicit guarantees as to the accuracy
of the information contained in this book and in some cases, names
of people and places have been altered to protect their privacy.

© 2007 Edward J. Laurie. All rights reserved.

No part of this book may be reproduced, stored in
a retrieval system, or transmitted by any means
without the written permission of the author.

First published by AuthorHouse 9/21/2007

ISBN: 978-1-4343-3108-3 (sc)

Printed in the United States of America
Bloomington, Indiana

This book is printed on acid-free paper.

For Meg
&
Kate
&
Beth

Prologue

I will be 82 this year and that means, as a good friend recently advised me, I will be running out of numbers one day soon and had best get on with anything I had in mind finishing. Otherwise, he suggested, it might turn out to be too late, as people in our age group seem to have an alarming habit of departing the planet on a regular and often sudden basis.

In retrospect, I think it rather that our children and grandchildren are seldom told tales of our own mischief as children. We stayed mum because we did not wish to encourage them in the equivalent of our own childhood misadventures.

For this small work I have decided to cover just the period from my first actual recollection as a person to my departure in June1943 from Sparks, Nevada, at the age of 17, to join the U. S. Navy in the middle of WWII which, for some inexplicable reason, has always been called 'the good war,' though I don't think there actually is any such thing. Perhaps they really mean a 'justified' war?

With most people living in cities these days, the small town ways of my memory may be disappearing and they have seriously changed since the period through the early1930s to the mid 1940s, if for no other reason than we have been marching along technologically and seem now to be embedded in a hasty and frantic time encouraged by a host of electronic communications devices, which often assist us in being Chicken Little writ large.

My childhood was conducted at a more leisurely pace than I see of children around me today. I believe they have lost much of what we once called 'childhood,' and I feel sorry for them. Time is of the very essence these days, even in childhood. That was not the case for those of us who grew up before WWII

We, it seems to me, simply aged, one day at a time, with our small traumas and adventures, in what were, though we were not that aware of it, 'pinching times,' as my mother often called them.

The most common phrase I remember, uttered by my mother, often in times of despair over the revelations of what I had been up to, was: 'Good grief, I'm rearing the Devil's own imp.' My father seemed to be of a similar opinion though he often put it somewhat more vulgarly.

Ed Laurie
March 31, 2007

The Elephant Trap

I have selected my tale of the elephant trap somewhat out of context because I believe it sets the character of all that follows in the book:

Way back in the late 1930's, an actor named Johnny Weismuller played the role of Tarzan. He was, in his day, the equivalent of Indiana Jones. It cost a dime to attend the Saturday afternoon matinees at the Sparks theatre. Having earned my way, by mowing lawns, I was a happy movie goer.

There were villains in Tarzan's jungle — people able to scale the Great Escarpment in search of gold, jewels and elephant tusks. Tarzan took a dim view of elephant traps. He did not seem concerned with jewels and gold, though fair maidens of various kinds, eternally and foolishly accompanying the nasty treasure hunters, required a rescue from time to time by that vine-swinging muscle man.

It was after one of Tarzan's successful adventures that I decided to trap an elephant of my own and acquire a set of tusks. Elephants were smart. They stuck to well-worn trails. Unless thoroughly enraged, they did not wander off their normal paths. An elephant visiting my immediate neighborhood, and possibly my yard, would obviously come up the back alley, open the gate and journey up the dirt path beside the wood shed — a large and ancient structure with bins for coal and wood and kindling. That was before we built the new garage.

Dad was frequently gone for weeks at a time. He worked for the Southern Pacific Railroad which sent him off to various parts of the state to keep him employed.

One of his extended fall absences provided the opportunity for digging the elephant trap. We had, in the shed, the requisite tools.

My mother was not one of those people who quite understood what to do with small boys. Often, she would say, 'Teddy, get out of the house and go and do whatever it is that little boys do.' I often did.

I began the patient digging of an elephant trap across the path alongside the shed. It was hard labor and took several days. The trap grew deep, eventually requiring a ladder for entry and exit. It was hard to get the dirt hurled upward and out of the way. At the later stages of the endeavor, the dirt had to be put in a pail, the ladder climbed, the contents dumped and the bucket returned to the bottom of the pit. But the prize of a set of elephant tusks encouraged every effort.

Eventually, the hard work was done. The hole stretched fully across the path, was three feet wide, six feet long and six feet deep. Just right, I thought, for trapping an elephant.

In the jungle, the nasty hunters would put sharpened bamboo shoots in the bottom of the pit to kill the elephant. Unfortunately, no bamboo grew in our neighborhood. I had to do the next best thing — drown the elephant. They are, as has been previously noted, smart. The great pile of dirt resulting from the hole had to be spread evenly in the vegetable garden to the rear of the yard and the left of the path. It was late fall. The frozen garden hose had to be thawed in the afternoon sun.

Caution! Elephants are very observant. The hose had to be buried in a trench leading from the back of our house to the elephant trap and covered with soil. In one or two places the trench went through the lawn. Grass sod had to be carefully dug up, the hose properly placed and the sod returned to make the trench through the lawn invisible.

Happily, a couple of vacant lots in the area were replete with willows. I cut a goodly crop and spread them across the open trap. Elephants are not blind. Soil, spread over the capping of willows made the trap, in anything except the harshest light, invisible.

It took several days to get the flow of water into the trap just right. Nevada has sandy soil and water can escape into the regions below. But with careful adjustments, I was able to keep a steady water level just below the willows. All was ready for the elephant, after I cautioned my sisters not to use the path at any hour, lest they get trapped inadvertently and drown.

It was the era of the Great Depression. Economy was always indicated. My father used a kerosene railroad lantern. In the name of thrift, it was his habit to shut off his lantern as soon as he reached familiar territory — his own alley, leading to his gate and own back yard. Light there was not necessary. No use to waste kerosene.

It was after ten o'clock one night, because I was listening to the Richfield reporter on the small radio in my room, when there was an enormous crash — my father had arrived home in something of an evil temper. I heard my mother say, 'Good heavens, Ted, you're soaking wet and muddy. What in the world happened to you?'

I heard my father's thundering voice, 'I tell you, Peggy, the little bastard's been trying to kill me for years! He damned near got me this time! I will kill him before he kills me!'

I presume he was headed for the stairs, but I heard my mother intervene, 'Now, now. You get yourself out of those wet clothes and into a hot tub of water. We'll have a bit of dinner and some tea, and discuss it.'

The Richfield Reporter droned on. I turned off the light and the radio and tucked myself deeply under the covers. Drat! Dad had utterly ruined my elephant trap. I would not be able to collect any ivory this time around. There would be difficulties in the morning, so it would be best to get a good night's sleep.

The morning had its grimmer elements. While Dad had calmed down considerably, I was seized by one ear, after breakfast, and instructed to let my trap drain of water, collect the soil I had spread around the vegetable garden, fill the hole, and dispose of the willows. This I did rapidly but reluctantly.

Further, since I seemed to enjoy digging, it would be wise if I spaded some of the grass that had been spread around the flower beds into the soil to act as mulch for spring planting. This I did with no objection.

The Spider Bite

One day, during my 16th year I mentioned to my mother that I'd had a dream about the time my sister Audrey had been bitten by a spider in Carlin, Nevada.

'That's not likely' my mother said. 'You were barely three years old when we moved from there to Sparks. You should not be able to remember a thing.'

'I don't remember the house we lived in,' I admitted. 'And I don't remember anything about Carlin, but I do remember the time Audrey and I were playing in the garage and she got bitten by a spider. She screamed and it scared me.'

Mother's brow wrinkled a bit and she admitted, 'Yes, she did get bitten by a spider, and it was in the garage behind the house in Carlin. She must have told you about it later. She was nearly six at the time.'

'I don't think she did,' I insisted, 'because I remember the garage very well. It was painted yellow and had twin doors and the one on the left was sagging off its hinges and two of the panes (there were four) of glass in the door were broken. The driveway was not paved, but made of white gravel, and I used to throw the prettier stones around.'

By now Mother grew genuinely interested. 'Do you remember anything else?'

'Yes,' I admitted. 'I remember there were two steamer trunks in the garage and one of them had a domed top. The other one was flat-topped, and Audrey was trying to crawl up on it when she got bitten by the spider. That was the reason she screamed.'

'I'm surprised, ' Mother admitted. 'Can you remember anything more?'

'Not much,' I said. 'It seems to me the railroad tracks were not very far from the back of the garage. I remember Dad marching us to the back and telling us we dare not go any further because of the tracks and the trains.'

I gave the matter more thought. 'The trains made an awful noise, and I was afraid of them, so I never did go beyond the back of the garage. At least I don't remember ever doing so.'

Mother probed a bit more. 'Do you remember anything else?'

'Well,' I said, 'I could be wrong, but I think Audrey wasn't wearing a dress, but a white blouse and some kind of red plaid skirt, and had on white sox, and there were shiny buckles on her shoes.'

My mother's eyebrows rose. 'I really do believe you remember. How odd! Most children don't recall anything at that age.'

'It was probably the spider,' I said.

'Yes,' she admitted, 'it probably was. But now it is time to make tea.'

My mother told me that when she and Dad first arrived in Nevada she was housed in a boxcar 'home' along the railroad tracks. She mentioned, often, it was not a pleasant place to live and they were fortunate to find the house in Carlin when they did.

Sparks, Nevada

I'd best shelve my personal adventures for a moment and tell you about Sparks in the early 1930s, then a very different place from what it is today.

When I left for the Navy, Sparks had a population of 7,500. According to the Internet, the current population is more than 90,000, so the town has turned into a small city and is now more than three times what Reno was in those days.

Reno was our neighboring city, 'The Biggest Little City in the World,' or so it was claimed by an iron sign arched across Virginia Street at the entrance to the main business district.

In my day Sparks was noted for but two oddities: (1) the entire business district was on the north side of the street with a mile-long park running along the southern side, and (2) the Southern Pacific Railroad had its division point there with a giant red-brick roundhouse at the eastern end of town. It was there that the great steam locomotives which pulled the long freight trains over the high Sierras were repaired and kept in shape.

On the southern side of the park, on 'A' Street, were the homes of the better-off folk of the town. They had only to cross 'A' Street, venture through the narrow park to 'B' Street to do their shopping.

'B' Street was paved from the eastern to the western end of town. Beyond, one encountered gravel roads until reaching the town of Lovelock. Then a paved street for a while, and then off on gravel again until Winnemucca, and so on across the state to Salt Lake City, Utah.

I have a vague memory of the early paving of 'Coney Island,' the 7-mile stretch from the west end of Sparks to Reno. Beyond Reno, some miles, the gravel roads triumphed again until one hit the California border. This made trips into the Sierras an adventure.

Before the great paving programs of the era of Franklin Roosevelt (the WPA and PWA), the main highway going east from Reno curved at our house, went south a few blocks, and then turned to the east again, becoming B Street.

A small ditch, running west/east separated our house from the highway. One of my vaguer memories is of floating little wooden rafts (pieces of the mill blocks that my dad bought for building kitchen fires) down that ditch until they hit a culvert which went under the highway. I was chastised on occasion for floating my older sister's dolls down the same stream on my 'rafts' and watching them disappear under the culvert never to be seen thereafter.

Again, I remember the garage rather than the house. There was a tree stump in the garage, much shredded at the top, which my dad used as a chopping block for making kindling. I also remember being instructed not to play with the hatchet which was kept very sharp and had its blade buried in the block when not in my dad's hands.

Of the house interior I can remember only the west living room wall with a doorway that led to the kitchen. There was a tiny, colored, flower clock with metal petals and a pendulum which hung on the wall to the left of the door and below it, a large phonograph which stood taller than I was, had a domed lid, and a crank on one side for winding the motor.

Sometimes I was allowed to turn the crank, but needed a small stool to reach it. I was also permitted to take a metal needle from a **counter-**sunk metal cup inside the top of the **machine and** replace the phonograph needle when needed.

Two of the songs that were often played on that machine were, 'My Blue Heaven,' and 'Red Sails in the Sunset.'

There was another song I enjoyed. It was about a fellow named Abdul Abul Bul Emir, who killed a fellow named Ivan Skavinsky Skavar.

I learned most of the lyrics of the song and can, with some accuracy I believe, give the first verse:

'By the sea of Sargossa I wandered one night.
The moon, it was shining quite clear.
For no reason at all,
I heard someone call for Abdul Abul Bul Emir.
Now Abdul Abul Bul I knew to be dead.
The story has spread near and far,
How he lost his life while plunging his knife
into Ivan Skavinsky Skavar.'

Mother played the record often in response of my requests. Accordingly, she claimed I was able to sing all of the verses of the song and did so frequently. Perhaps, but I certainly didn't know what a Hussar was and quite forgot to ask. Much later, the song was revived by Bert Parks and became a hit again. If you wait long enough everything familiar may return.

At the front of the house there were small concrete steps leading directly from the living room which had a screened door as well as a regular one. The screen door opened outward, the front door inward. I'm certain of this, because I had to move from my favorite perch (the steps) to let people come and go. I liked to sit there because I could watch the trucks go by on the highway on their way to Reno or to the east.

My Airplane

I received my airplane the Christmas of 1930 when I had turned five. It was a small metal affair with stubby wings, probably not more than a foot in length, a cockpit, and pedals inside the cockpit for pumping.

The red brick duplex next door had a sloping driveway which was just the thing for gaining speed with my airplane in the hope that it would fly. To my disappointment, it never did. It had a propeller in the front which spun around as I pedaled along.

I was riding around in my airplane for a long while the day my younger sister, Shirley, was born. Apparently, I had been out too long because I wet my pants. When this was discovered, I was roughly hauled into the house by a Mrs. Jacobs, the midwife nurse who had been hired for mother's labor and delivery. She stripped off my clothes (to my horror and embarrassment), wiped me down with a wet cloth and put me to bed with a savage shake or two.

From that moment on, I hated the woman even though I had to be polite, if distant, when I went to her house, because her son was the local dentist and had his office at the front of the place. I detest the memory of the woman to this day.

The birth of my sister was not, fortunately, associated directly my accident, though there may have been some kind of psychological connection. To be honest, I don't remember that much about her until she became fully mobile some years later. In the meantime, I had an older sister to deal with on a daily basis.

The Purloined Bird Cage

One day a new family moved into the brick duplex next door. That was the place with the marvelous sloping driveway. In the process, they laid out a number of things on the sidewalk as they were moving in.

One of the items intrigued me. It was a birdcage which I promptly acquired and marched happily into our house.

'Where did you get that cage?' Mother asked.

'I made it,' I said.

Mother queried, 'Where in the world did you get the wire?'

'At the junk yard,' I lied.

'The junk yard is more than two miles from here,' Mother observed, 'and you haven't been gone that long. Now, young man, where did you get the birdcage?'

'I found it on the street.'

'Where?'

'Well, on the sidewalk.'

'Next door I presume.'

'Yes.'

'Take it back at once, and if they ask how you came by it, apologize!'

She cast her eyes toward heaven and sighed: 'I'm rearing the Devil's own child.' It was a phrase I was destined to hear rather often.

Though my illegal acquisition of the bird cage failed, it puzzled me seriously how my own mother could doubt for a moment that I made the birdcage myself, wires, roosts, little sliding door and all. It seemed, at the time, like the best and most logical explanation of my sudden new found prize.

And, thinking it over on the way to return the cage, I should have suggested that I got to the city dump and back so quickly because I flew in my airplane. For one reason or another, I thought better of it.

The Soda Pop Stand

Our new neighbors included Mr. and Mrs. Lightfoot whose son, Don, became my playmate and friend for many years thereafter. Mrs. Lightfoot's mother (Mrs. McGee) and her sister

(Barbara McGee) resided in the other side of the duplex.

Mrs. McGee and I got along famously. She was elderly, played solitaire all day, and smoked through a cigarette holder constantly. She had a card table set up in her living room and it became my privilege, when watching her at solitaire, to remove the stub of a cigarette from the holder, pull out a small piece of stained cotton using a toothpick, put fresh cotton in its place, and then insert the new cigarette. I became very good at this, and was always thanked, and then given lessons about how to play one or two of the simpler varieties of solitaire to which I eventually became addicted.

Mrs. Lightfoot, Don's mother, and I did not get along as well. Mother once remarked it might be because I was doing better in school than Don. Don got 'C' grades and I got 'A' grades, or it may have been just one of those personality things.

It did not matter. Don and I never held any intellectual discussions of any kind. We were about a host of other small-boy adventures which had to do with playing with our toy cars (in those days, pot metal, not plastic) and making roads for them in an empty lot or, after aging a bit, digging tunnels or camping out in his new and larger back yard, or playing 'Run Sheep Run,' or baseball, or going swimming in the Truckee River.

One morning I wandered from the front concrete steps out to our backyard and noticed that the fellow who had erected a soda pop stand (a small wooden affair to the north and west of our garage) had built a bonfire to clear up some brush in the area. The fire, it seemed to me, was awfully close to his stand. A breeze had come up and the flames were blowing in that direction as he was engrossed in conversation with a fellow in a car that had pulled up beside the stand.

I trotted around our house and found Mrs. Lightfoot in her front yard.

'The man who runs the soda pop stand has built a fire, and it is close to his stand. I think it will burn up.'

'Oh, Teddy,' Mrs. Lightfoot said, 'you're such an imaginative little liar. Go home and don't be bothering me.'

So I did as ordered. I went home and parked myself on the concrete steps in front and waited. Eventually, there were sirens and a fire truck came by, and then another one.

Mr. Lightfoot, hearing the excitement, rushed into his back yard, joined his hose to ours, and tried to get near the fire. Even then I must have intuitively known something about physics, because I knew he would never, with the elongated hose, get sufficient water pressure to be of any help. Moreover, he was using his thumb to create a spray (rather than a legitimate nozzle as my father used) so, in the end, his help was fruitless.

As I had earlier observed, the soda-pop stand burnt to the ground.

Eventually, I walked up to Mrs. Lightfoot, who was attending to the excitement, fixed her with what I supposed to be a harsh stare, and said, 'I told you so!'

'What was that all about?' Mr. Lightfoot asked, having given up his own efforts.

'Nothing important,' she said, giving me the kind of return glare that meant silence on my part would be wise.

I never clashed with Mrs. Lightfoot after that, and since Don and I were constant buddies, she held her peace and I held mine. I did not know the proper word then, but in retrospect I think 'detente' fits nicely.

Much later, when the fire had been fully put out, the firemen gone, and the neighborhood clear of intrigued observers, Don and I snuck back to the place and found some bottles of still warm soda pop. We drank them and later got thoroughly sick from 'unknown causes.'

Whatever we were up to, the one rule we always followed was that we did not 'rat' on each other. We had our own code of the west, and like our heroes Tom Mix and Charles Starrett, kept our six guns handy and our shadier activities hidden.

Trains and Magazines

While Mrs. Lightfoot and I may have reached a détente, I would have to admit that both of Don's parents were enormously tolerant of the activities, in and out of the house, of two small boys. Perhaps that was because Don was an only child?

We were allowed, the two of us, to erect train tracks for Don's freight train through his bedroom, the living room, the dining room, and sometimes even parts of the kitchen. Mrs. Lightfoot would wend her way through all this without remark and/or complaint. Most wonderfully, Donald was allowed to leave the tracking in place for several days, something that would never have been readily permitted by my mother.

Our bridges and tunnels were made from books and they too could be left in place over fairly long periods of time.

Mr. Lightfoot was a fan of the National Geographic. Beside his leather reading chair in the living room were great stacks of the magazine. Sometimes when Don was about some other business, I would sit in Mr. Lightfoot's chair and pour through them. Thus I traveled to various foreign lands, complete with pictures of the natives and their odd activities.

Don was not himself a reader. Quite often he would wander off into the yard as I poured through many of the magazines. On occasion, Mrs. Lightfoot would find me in Mr. Lightfoot's chair reading and would say, 'Good grief, Teddy. I didn't know you were still here. I think it is time you went home for dinner.' It usually was.

Frequently, our train adventures would require that I stay overnight. This was great because in the morning Don and I were fed cups of hot chocolate and well-buttered toast which we were permitted to dunk into the hot chocolate. Delicious!

At my house this would have been a luxury, since we did not own an automatic pop-up toaster and hot chocolate was not a common breakfast item.

The Parrot

A parrot is a wondrous creature when you are very young and ridden with innocence. Since it can talk as you do, the assumption is that it's a very intelligent creature indeed. But I had an even greater reason for that assumption.

The parrot was owned by a Mrs. Williams (a widow who lived two houses to the south of us). She had a screened front porch which contained a very large bird cage and the aforementioned parrot.

Mrs. Williams was apparently the second owner of the bird because his name was 'Salty,' and he seemed to favor three words, 'Avast,' 'Ahoy,' and 'Hello.'

In retrospect I believe Mrs. Williams had a wicked sense of humor, was an excellent teacher, and had a lot of time on her hands.

It was not very long before, when visiting the parrot (which, fascinated, I did often), he would say, 'Hello Teddy,' or 'Avast Teddy,' or 'Ahoy Teddy.' He seemed to have no particular preference in the matter of the use of the terms and was often repetitious. That did not matter. I talked to him often and at length and sometimes told him my troubles.

Mrs. Williams, by the way, liked to bake, and my second reward for a visit, beyond the joy of the parrot, was that I was almost always presented with a cookie or two, peanut butter most often.

It was not all that long before the parrot would not only say, 'Hello Teddy,' or 'Ahoy Teddy,' but chimed up to my fondest needs and would say, 'Teddy wants a cookie. Teddy wants a cookie!'

Since the parrot always got one too, I now believe he had his own interests at heart. But, at five years of age, I assumed he was thinking of me.

I suppose every joy has its sorrow and even rapture has its descent.

It so happened that Mrs. Williams was not only gifted with a parrot but a red ant hill just to the right of her front porch which, I had the singular misfortune one day, to stand on.

The result of that choice was that I was soundly and badly stung on both legs which resulted in a rescue by Mrs. Williams, a washing down of my legs, mostly below the knees, and the application of some kind of pink lotion to ease the pain of all those welts, in the meantime accompanied by running commentary from the parrot, who remained much more concerned about my getting a cookie.

I continued to visit the parrot anyway, but always stayed on the front walk on the way to the front porch. The bitten child is suitably wary. I did think it unkind that the Salty did not warn me about ants.

Stilts

In the house beyond the parrot lived two undisciplined (the word 'delinquent' was not used in those days) high school boys of the last name of Parker. They were of the adventurous sort, and there were always remarks of a scornful nature by adults about, 'those Parker boys!'

They were into stilts — very tall ones — and caves. There was a quality of real daring-do about those two. I cannot remember either of their first names. But they were an entertainment to those of us of wide-eyes and young years.

I remember they built stilts of great height such that the two of them, walking around the neighborhood, could move into a yard and sit on the edge of a roof of the house of their choice before they moved on with long strides like circus clowns. They were, as nearly as I could tell, masters of the heights and also of balance. I never saw either of them take a fall.

After watching their antics, my sister and I made suitable pleas to my father to build us stilts too. He did, but they were of a very disappointing height comparatively speaking. Mine were such that they raised my feet not more than a foot or two, if that, from the ground. What is more, they were not the kind that were strapped to the legs, but rather the kind with tall poles that reached up above your arms for holding. Not quite the daring-do I had in mind. Still, they were fun, and my sister and I both enjoyed them.

I remember too that the footrests were bordered by pieces of garden hose nailed such that we could insert our feet and they would not slide off the edges but left room enough for a quick exit of the foot to cushion a fall, of which there were plenty earlier on.

The Parker boys on the other hand had no such addition to their foot braces and did not need them, because their stilts ended just below the knee and their legs and feet were held securely by belt straps — much more sophisticated, and, as my father opined rather loudly when I had pointed this out, 'much more dangerous.'

If you haven't guessed already, I should mention that the Parker boys, equally attracted by my parrot friend, chose Mrs. Williams's porch roof as their most frequent roosting place. For one thing it was the easiest place to sit being rather flatter than most roofs and, for a second, they could teach the parrot things that Mrs. Williams did not wish him to say.

But she got her revenge in her own way. She often would say, 'those Parker boys will come to a bad end. They are bad boys.'

Accordingly, the parrot often greeted the boys, as they roosted on his roof with 'bad boys,' 'bad boys,' or 'bad end,' 'bad end.'

I don't recall whether the Parker lads ever asked for or received any cookies. Certainly Salty never asked for any for them. It is a wise bird who knows his owner.

'I will make myself stilts like that one day,' I remarked to my dad as the boys departed the neighborhood with giant strides. 'I'm sure you will,' he nodded, 'but not until you are at least as old as they are.' To me that seemed to be down the road an infinite distance.

As for caves, that was a different matter. There were, as in most small towns, various empty lots about. There was one in the block immediately behind the Parker house and it was there that the boys, abjuring stilts from time to time, dug tunnels which I presume they roofed with various timbers 'borrowed' from a lumber yard several blocks away.

They invited me into their tunnel system one afternoon. I'm sure the tunnels were not as deep, or as long, or quite as dark, as they seemed to me when I was lured into them. But the boys had pieces of candle to light the way.

To me it was a wonderful adventure into the unknown, as I duly reported when I got home. But, unfortunately, there was hell to pay. My mother marched her way to the Parker house and had much to say to the two boys in question. To my regret, I was never invited into the tunnels thereafter. I did hear later that the system had eventually collapsed and had to be filled in. I thought that a great pity.

I should mention that after their high school graduation, something of a miracle in itself, as oft remarked, the Parker boys enlisted in the United States Marines. They returned to Sparks a couple of times in shining uniforms. I presume they later participated in WWII, and it is my certainty they were bold and brave, and my private hope they survived.

Odd Boy Out

Being the odd boy out is not easy. It became noticeable when I was delivered, at the age of five, to kindergarten. I watched events for a while and when recess came and ended, I moved myself into Miss Mulaney's first grade class on my own volition. Miss Mulaney was not expecting an after-recess addition to her class and made inquiries about what I was doing there and why I had arrived.

I explained that I could read and write (the latter but a little) and it seemed to me, I explained, that kindergarten was on the order of playtime, and I had expected school was about serious work.

I was asked for a demonstration, and so read all the words on all the ugly green cards circling the room above the blackboards. I also enforced my case by reading from the first-grade reader. Accordingly, I was delivered to the principal's office for consultation. The end result was that Mr. Diltz decided to let me remain in the first grade and my parents were duly informed.

It seemed a good idea at the time, but being the class dwarf for the next twelve years was not all that rewarding. Perhaps if both my parents had not been taller, I could have overcome the difficulty. It was not to be. Even at the end, the high school dances were embarrassing since there were only two girls of less than my limited height and I did not particularly like either of them. Still, one adapted and made do.

I would correct an old and absurd axiom: 'It's not the size of the dog in the fight, but the size of the fight in the dog.' It sounds great. Bah! Humbug! When the other dog in the fight is one foot taller and thirty pounds heavier, he is going to win, and you are going to lose. You can lose even if you are in a state of absolute rage and he is merely 'horsing around.' I believe it has something to do with the laws of physics.

Once I did forget the rules of physics. We had a junior high bully a few blocks away who liked to torment the small grammar school boys wending their way home. One of the unfortunates he often lay in wait for was me. I endured a lot of abuse for a long time and then, just once, snapped.

While being punched and tormented by Curtis M., I finally retaliated and seized him by the throat and hung on through all his physical gyrations until he fell to the ground unconscious. Still in a rage, I hauled him to the lot my dad had recently purchased and which he was ridding of rocks. This meant the existence of a large pit toward the street where the rocks would be put and then covered over.

I tossed Curtis, still apparently unconscious, into the pit and began to cover him with the extra rocks that were at hand until I was interrupted by Mr. Griffin who lived across the street. Curtis was hauled to his feet, shaken into recovery, and sent on his way.

'That was a bit too much, I think,' Mr. Griffin remarked. 'But I don't think he'll be tormenting you anymore.' Mr. Griffin was right. Curtis kept his distance thereafter. A wise decision too, because I was still seething with rage.

The Publisher

I have always been fascinated with printing and publication. It started when I was very young. As soon as I had learned to read and write, I asked for a 'Tom Thumb' typewriter for Christmas.

It was basically a toy. At the top of the mechanism was a wheel with the letters of the alphabet and also numbers. I had to dial the wanted letter or number and then push a large lever to print it on the paper which fitted into the machine. There was a small purple ink pad inside which inked the characters, and a small bottle for re-inking the pad. All the letters were upper case, of course.

I promptly went about the business of creating a neighborhood newspaper. I don't know how long it took me to produce the first six one-page copies of my news. I do recall that they were confiscated immediately after they had been distributed, and my toy typewriter was also confiscated for a week until I had solemnly sworn not to print any further news that would embarrass the family. Memory does not serve me well in the matter of the content of my first publication. I can't imagine that it was very spicy — not at that early age.

I wore out the Tom Thumb typewriter eventually, but by some magic, my dad found an old Corona portable typewriter with a real ribbon, a real platen, and real keys to strike. I also remember that it folded in half and that it had a shift key for capital letters and also a shift key for numbers. The whole upper half of the machine rose for capital letters and even higher for numbers.

When I was in the first grade, I vanished from Miss Mulhaney's class for a while. There was a search, and I was eventually discovered in the office of the Principal Mr. Diltz — he was not about at the time. I was sitting at his desk writing something or other on his typewriter.

Mr. Diltz was a remarkable man. I was not punished. Rather, I was told I could come into the office during recess and use the typewriter if I wanted. Also, I was permitted to do the same for a half hour after the school day ended.

In the 10th grade I enrolled in a typing class and really took to the operation of such machines. At least I got an 'A' and went on to the advanced class and got another one. This, naturally, led to my working on the high school newspaper — 'The Streamliner.'

In the latter part of my junior year I had to come to a great decision. I could continue on the basketball team, though I was hardly a star and spent most of my time on the bench, or I could become the editor of 'The Streamliner.' I chose the newspaper route. The coach never quite forgave me. At least he was seldom civil after that. In those days, height was important for a center or a guard, but not for a forward, particularly, if he had a fairly reliable hook shot. Fast dribbling and swift movement were more important than height in those days. Things have changed.

For the job of editor one had to be able to write reasonably well and also proofread with some skill — alas for the latter long-gone talent.

Does anyone remember the mimeograph, and the tedious work creating stencils, and all those styli that were required for art work, then inking the pad carefully, if one wanted to do color work which, due to leakage around the edges, was somewhat fuzzy, but glorious fun?

Ink Wells

I recall my early classroom days, when the desks and seats were one piece — the seat anchored to the desk behind and made of oak, the desk equipped with a lift-up lid.

The inkwells I encountered were not the type for dipping pigtails — the girls of the time were wearing Shirley Temple curls. And the wells were countersunk in that narrow forward part of the desk that did not lift. They had sliding caps on them and the uncovered hole was just large enough to insert the pen nib. The pens were made of polished, redwood and the points were interchangeable. One dipped and wrote, dipped and wrote. We did not do that very often, only for English themes, because this involved smoother, lined, paper which was passed out for that special occasion.

Just why the ink paper was replete with lines and the pencil paper not so, was never explained, nor can I recollect making any queries about the anomaly.

Ink wells dried out from time to time, and the teacher made a trip around the room on those days demanding themes and filled the wells from a tall bottle with a thin spout at the top. Otherwise, we made do with eraser-less pencils of similar wood, and a light tan paper that came in two sizes, 12' x 9' or 9' x 6'.

We were never permitted to take home any of the ink paper, but could always take home a quarter inch or so of the tan paper for homework, particularly math.

The brown paper made passable airplanes of either the square or pointed variety. The English theme paper did make better airplanes but was generally not available, save as we sometimes rescued used sheets from the classroom wastebasket, or converted our own returned themes to more practical uses. As a result, many a theme achieved a physical altitude beyond its literary worth.

Most of the desk tops were well-carved with the initials of former occupants, or adorned with messages in ink, or deeply scribed in pencil — not the best of surfaces for writing. But, from time to time, when they were disgracefully scarred, they suffered a summer sanding and varnishing and were smooth as glass for the next lucky class.

The desks had attached forward seats, except at the front of the room where they stood alone, or in the back, where a second desk tailed behind, seat-less and provided double storage for those lucky enough to bring up the rear. The desks were held together by fancy, black, wrought iron frames.

They were also bolted directly (in rows) to long slats that ran the length of the room from back to near the teacher's desk. They did not move about, though they did vibrate if the fellow seated in front of you happened to be a wiggle wart.

Order was the mode of the day. And, of course, seating was always alphabetic, which meant I was always in the middle of the room and Billy Zenclusen was always in the back where he could maximize his potential for mischief, which was considerable. Alden Arnold always had one of the front seats and deeply resented the close watch on his own would-be impieties.

The blackboards were black then, made of some kind of sturdy slate, with the occasional long crack running top to bottom. The chalk rails were broad and accommodated puffy erasers with the hard backs which sometimes got involved in hall fights. This was frowned upon.

The American flag was always to the teacher's right in the front corner of the room. Each morning, we were required to stand and recite the Pledge of Allegiance which, in those days, was not under God — President Eisenhower had him inserted later. Something about the majesty of the flag salute in the morning had the force of an immediate call to order.

Grim fading green portraits of President Washington and President Lincoln hung on the front wall, high up, behind the teacher's desk. They were a septic green, as I recall. Or had they been there so long as to turn that grim color? I don't remember a classroom at the Robert Mitchell Grammar school without their steel-eyed green supervision.

Our classroom floors were made of heavy pine and oiled at least once a week by the janitor — more than likely over the weekend.

On Mondays there might be an oil puddle here and there and slippery, so suitable cautions were announced about not running in the halls.

The playground was a basic affair. There were chain-hung swings of sturdy wood which caused the occasional injury if one did not stay alert and nimble.

There were 'monkey bars,' a steel ladder suspended in the air by runged steel posts. Up, up, and across! The larger boys skipped a rung per each swing and presented a constant dare to those of us who were smaller to do likewise. This often resulted in falls to the ground which, as is normal in a well-trampled arena, was as hard as rock. In the spring and summer a great fog of dust hung over the place.

We had a slide, decently large and with one concession to softness — a sand-filled pit at the bottom. But naturally, we speeded things up.

'Store-bought' bread came in waxed paper in those days. A slide could be 'greased' to a fare-thee-well by sitting on the opened bread wrapper and sliding down. This done frequently, a slide trip went faster than a speeding bullet with the result that we were often hurled out of the sand pit onto its wooden frame producing bruises and other minor injuries.

Schoolyard hazards and injuries were expected by students, by teachers, by parents and by administrators. Unless the injuries were serious — and they seldom were — one was patched up by a teacher or, if she happened to be visiting on that day, a school nurse, and that was an end to it. One sported a firmly anchored, bulky bandage of gauze and for the rest of the day — a badge of honor for daring.

The Robert Mitchell School had a most pleasant fence about the front lawn. It was made of three-foot posts through which three iron pipes had been inserted horizontally. These presented opportunities for climbing, sitting and sometimes falling. A backward fall was relatively safe because of the lawn. A forward fall was a bit more dangerous thanks to the sidewalks around the school and yard which, by the way, occupied an entire city block.

One of our favorite stunts was to raid the teacher's wastebasket immediately after class and save up used pen nibs. We hoarded them a while and then, during recess, snuck our pen holders out of the classroom.

A telephone pole occupied the southwest corner of the school yard and was an ideal target for hurled pens. Someone with a pocket knife had carved a series of rings in the pole. Our challenge was to hit the bull's-eye and win a nib. My aim being rotten, I wound up providing most of my scrounged nibs to the other contestants.

The student desks grew with us as we moved annually from class to higher class — those of us that passed, that is, and not all did then as now. Whatever their size, their bins seemed commodious but were ultimately stuffed to the limit during the school year.

In early June, the last day of classes was not for learning, but for cleaning. We could not receive our report cards until our desks had been emptied and inspected. On that day, by some miracle of adult planning, each classroom was suddenly equipped with a large, galvanized garbage pail.

One poked around in his cluttered desk — it took a while — discovered missing wonders, such as long-lost steelies or aggies and the missing Swiss or Scout knife, and filled one's pockets with that which was to be preserved at home during the joyous days of summer.

Or, as in the case of Billy Z., a couple of long-dead 'horny' toads showed up and had to be discarded to the accompaniment of shrieks of horror by most of the girls.

The galvanized garbage pail filled to the brim, the desks thoroughly inspected, extra paper and pencils and pens once more secure in the teacher's cabinet, we marched, one at a time, to the front of the room, were handed our report cards and wished, sometimes even with a smile, a pleasant summer and perhaps a more productive next year. Whether or not the next year would be better was at best debatable.

The Ichthyopatolite

It may have begun with goldfish and Oreo cookies. In Sparks, we walked the several blocks to the Robert Mitchell Grammar School (K-6). There were always things of interest on the way.

One lady had an outdoor fishpond in her front yard replete with those expensive golden carp they are so fond of in China and Hawaii. To me, of course, they were merely very large and very interesting goldfish. Whenever I went close to the pool, the fish seemed to line up as if in expectation of some treat that might come their way. It seemed to me, since I had an abiding affection for Oreo cookies, the fish would find them tasty too.

So, one day, on the way to school, I gave them (having filched a surplus larger than what my mother intended) a feast. They seemed content enough. But, duly, they died and the lady who owned them arrived at our doorstep in some indignation to complain. I recall her saying to my mother, 'I know. I know. With that golden hair and large brown eyes, he looks like an angel, but he's not!'

'Teddy is well behaved,' my Mother insisted.

'He should be named Terrible Teddy,' the indignant woman countered.

My dad, sitting through the conversation remained pensive. Perhaps he sensed his future hazards with the elephant trap or my Egyptian tomb period.

Having defended her offspring and having sent the unhappy fish owner on her way, my mother once again lifted her eyes to heaven and said, 'It's true. I am rearing the devil's own imp.'

A Language Problem

Whilst I was waiting to attend grammar school, I learnt to speak the English language. This, it turned out, was not American. Accordingly, to my surprise, my 'whilst' and 'learnt' were marked down as spelling errors. I was indignant and said so, but my teachers were implacable. I would write 'while' and 'learned' and that was it! Too, I would learn to convert 'lift' to 'elevator,' and so on.

One does learn more quickly under peer pressure. It did not take me very long, when playing cars with friend Don and others to convert 'boot,' 'bonnet,' and 'windscreen' to 'trunk,' 'hood,' and 'windshield.

There were many other words of that sort which fouled up my spelling grades until I got the hang of it. I did learn, somewhere along the line, not to say that I was going to 'knock up' a girl friend. In England that meant you might visit her and rap on her door. In America, that would mean you'd gotten her pregnant. Now, that's a *really big* difference, such as between a friendly encounter and a shotgun wedding!

I might also add that my clear enunciation was thought to be a bit pompous. And there was the other matter of accenting syllables so that my 'controversy' had an accent on the wrong syllable. It is a solid lesson to learn that right is often a matter of habit and/or choice. This makes one, I believe, more tolerant and flexible in the long run.

Even to this day I remind myself that anyone who speaks with an accent knows at least two languages. Well, so do I, but they are both versions of English.

In the main I now do things the American way, though the occasional 'whilst' and/or 'learnt' pop up in my writings unexpectedly.

Ah well, my dad, a Canadian, always noted that Americans sounded as though they were talking through tin cans. His 'aboot' was our 'about.'

Eventually, he surrendered to the common weal. Mother never did. 'Proper,' in her view, was never open to negotiation.

First Move

It was never explained to me why we moved from the small yellow house along the highway to the first house on 'C' Street, but I suppose it was because, with the birth of my younger sister, the other place was no longer deemed large enough to accommodate the family.

The new rental on 'C' Street was the middle of three identical houses built sometime around 1900.

I remember the day we moved into the second house because Mother, faced with a kitchen wainscot that had been painted a brilliant orange, sat down on the bare and neglected pine floor and cried.

My dad insisted he would repaint the wainscot, and the whole kitchen for that matter, to her taste. Further, he noted, he would sand and paint the worn kitchen floor and pick up a suitable piece of 'linoleum' for covering the most of it. Dad always kept his promises.

The house had two bedrooms, a kitchen, a small living room, a bathroom, a front unscreened porch with a sloping floor and little else that I can remember.

Dad spent his time at home clearing weeds out of the neglected front and back yards and burning the debris. He also planted new grass.

The house next door, and furthest from the corner was, by comparison, a much more elegant place surrounded by a white picket fence, with a rich green lawn front and back, with wooden planked walkways to the front of the house and from the back to a tool shed and a larger wood shed. Its porch was screened to keep out the summer insects. It was owned by a Mr. Englekey and had been expanded by the addition of two attic rooms with small dormers projecting from the roof north and south and a larger dormer to the east.

A Home of Our Own

One day Dad walked into our rented house and told my mother that, their two sons fully grown and having departed, Mr. and Mrs. Englekey were getting a divorce, and he had bought the house with a loan from the FHA.

Dad always credited Mr. Roosevelt with the achievement, but based on other facts, I think it was just before Mr. Roosevelt became President.

Mother was pleased, my older sister and I delighted. It seemed such a neat and green place, and well-cared for, and my older sister and I (my younger sister still an infant) would have our own upstairs rooms. What a wonder! What a delight!

'Well,' my dad said to my mother, the day we moved in, 'at last we have a home of our own again!'

I learned later that when he and Mother had originally married, he and Grandpa Laurie had built a home for the newlyweds, and it was not until my Uncle Chuck told Dad things would be more prosperous in Nevada (which proved untrue), that Dad sold that house and came south.

He had been born at Miller's siding in North Dakota as Grandma and Grandpa Laurie were on their way from New York City where they had landed, to Cranbrook, B.C. where my Grandpa intended to work for the Canadian Pacific Railroad.

After I had completed my fascination with the stairs that led from the kitchen to the attic rooms, I explored my new quarters; a small affair with a bed, a little square stand next to it, a four-drawer dresser, a padded window seat, and the dormer overlooking the back yard, where a twin-planked path through the grass led to the small tool shed on the left and the larger, much older wood shed to the right.

I also had a curtained closet which led to the lowest possible corner of the attic so that odd things of small size could be cramped back there and quickly forgotten.

My sister's room was somewhat larger, and when my younger sister was out of the crib, she joined my older sister there. That room had two beds and two dressers and a somewhat larger closet.

It was the window seat in my room which I most enjoyed. It was padded and had a hinged lid revealing a storage box of some capacity underneath. There I stored my special treasures, including a number of my favorite books.

The window seat was a place where I was never alone. I met David Copperfield, Nero Wolfe, Hercule Poirot, Miss Marple, Reggie Fortune, Ahab and Starbuck, Penrod, Huckleberry Finn, Tom Sawyer, Toby Tyler of circus fame, Sidney Carlton, Dorothy and the Wizard and all her odd friends, Oliver Twist, Robinson Crusoe, Horatio Nelson, George Washington, Benjamin Franklin, Abraham Lincoln, Long John Silver, The Little Match Girl, Ali Baba, Mr. Toad, and an endless stream of other fascinating people who, sadly, have never been introduced to the last two generations.

On that window seat I traveled to Egypt, to India, to Rome, to England, to Scotland, to Africa and ventured through time from the Egyptians, through the Greeks, to the Romans, and to the Persian Empire.

Four decades later, I sat there again, a few months before my father sold the house, and some of the stories seemed to pass through my mind as fresh as ever.

The Company

Dad went to work with the Southern Pacific Railroad Company when he was 24. He worked as a machinist, then a brakeman, and finally, having gathered enough seniority, as a conductor, moving eventually from freight trains to passenger trains, though he always claimed to prefer the freight trains — larger toys for older boys. He wound up as conductor on the streamlined 'City of San Francisco' until his heart attack at the age of 69 and his subsequent forced retirement.

When he was displeased, which was rare, Dad referred to the Southern Pacific Railroad Company as simply, 'The Company.' Otherwise, he just called it the 'SP.'

The company dominated our lives. We had a telephone to be sure, but it was largely reserved for receiving calls to work because Dad was on the 'extra board.' We were on a party line at first, but that changed quickly due to 'gabby females,' as Dad labeled them. He wanted no interference with notices for work.

We were commanded to make any of our calls short and businesslike, and so we did. This was the reverse of modern teenage life.

The SP tracks were two blocks south of our house, running east and west. Trains were, and are, heavy and noisy. When a long freight went from east to west, or the other way, our house vibrated as the trains roared by. It gave me a continuing sense, during childhood, of their great weight and importance. I always suspected that's why the minor earthquakes first encountered when I came to California, barely came to my attention, and left me somewhat surprised at the terror they seemed to bring to others. This remains so to this day.

My earlier childhood was still the age of steam. I could lie in my bed at night — my dormer window faced south in the direction of the tracks — and listen to the chuff-hiss, chuff-hiss of the switch engines working in the switch yard. Sometimes, if the engineer was a novice or inattentive, the wheels would slip and there would be a flurry of chuff-chuff-chuff hisses as balance between rail and spinning wheels was sought.

More fascinating, was to walk over to the railroad yard to watch the great locomotives being assembled to drag a mile-long freight over the high Sierras. Two huge engines were placed in front, and sometimes, one in the middle, and always another in the rear. It took something in the way of superb coordination between the engineers to get off to an even start, never perfectly achieved. There would be a great deal of hissing as the steam valves released boiler pressure that had grown too high.

During really heavy weather, such as the winter of 1937, the great snowplow engines, with their huge frontal, spinning, snow blades, would leave

Sparks and head into the Sierras spewing great streams of snow to one side as they moved along.

Sometimes, on a rare winter trip to Galena Creek in the lower Sierras, or Donner Lake, one could watch the engines laboring along the side of a high granite cliff, spewing snow to the depths below.

There were also long wooden snow sheds along the Sierra route. Sometimes one would collapse from the snow load and there would be delays on the road. It was a constant matter of pride and challenge for the railroad men to get their trains from Sparks to Sacramento. After the mountains, as Dad used to say, 'it was an easy coast to Oakland.' From Oakland one boarded a ferry boat which took one to the Ferry Building in San Francisco.

Most appealing, later on, when I was in junior high, was the rushing by of the famous streamliner, the 'City of San Francisco.' It nightly thundered through Sparks on its way east to Lovelock and beyond, sending the mournful sound of its deep horn rolling across the desert country.

I would lie in bed and dream of all the rich and important people headed east who were on important business that justified so luxurious a ride.

In 1939, near Carlin, Nevada the streamliner was moving around a bend at 100 mph when the track gave way and the train collided with a steel trestle. Cars were strewn helter-skelter across the desert and 109 people died. It was said to be sabotage, but the matter was never convincingly settled.

Dad ultimately had pictures of the wreckage. Later, toward the end of his career, he was the conductor for that same train. I secretly worried about it, but never said anything. Actually, he preferred the freights to the passenger trains — he was not happy with chores of dealing with passengers and their demands when there was a train to operate.

We were taught, from the very beginning, to respect the mighty weight of a railroad train and how long it took one to come to a halt. I loved to visit the massive roundhouse at the east end of Sparks where the giant locomotives were repaired and maintained. I was always cautioned, because there were as many as twenty parallel tracks in the switching yard, to pay sharp attention and never stand on the rails — 'keep a decent distance,' Dad would always warn.

One time, visiting the switch yard, I did get caught between two tracks and two switch engines moving cars about it — 'making up a train,' as they said. I did as instructed; I stood in the center between the tracks and closed my eyes so as not to be made dizzy by the bidirectional movement about me. The trains were moving slowly, so there was no high-speed suction, as when very fast trains pass each other on parallel tracks. That, I have never experienced.

On rare occasion, 'Speed' Henry, one of the senior hog heads (engineers), would let me mount into the locomotive cab and would give me a short ride from the east-end yards to the west-end station — the length of Sparks. The station was almost directly opposite our house a street or two to the south. When you are young, that's as close to a heavenly adventure as you can get.

I never got a chance to sit in the cabin of one of the giant engines. They were always about more important business than switching, and the operation was too dedicated and too serious for recreational adventures or 'civilian' entertaining.

The railroad, then, was part and parcel of my life, during my day and all through my nights. The sounds and sights had a strong influence on my hopes and dreams. Names like Huntington, Sherman, Stanford and Crocker were not entirely unfamiliar, though such remarks as accompanied those names — amongst the railroad workers at least — were often profane and had a lot to do with the alleged illegitimacy of their several births.

Sandy

When I was nine or ten, Dad brought him home, a puppy in a fancy wooden cage with the name 'Sandy' engraved on the top with one of those old-time wood-burning wands. He was soft, friendly and furry, and he was mine. There is no greater love than a boy for his own dog.

Sandy did not stay a puppy all that long. His mother turned out to have been an English Shepherd and his father a St. Bernard. True to his genes, Sandy grew, and grew, and grew. He also ate, and ate, and ate.

Dad made a shoulder harness for him to which I could hitch a light chain. Then, on my roller skates, I could be pulled down those rare Sparks sidewalks at enormous speed. It was my answer to the motorized skateboard which did not exist at the time. Rounding a fast corner, Sandy would cut inward and I would swing outward connected by the chain.

Our local sheriff, a rather rotund fellow, was walking the business streets one day, comfortable in his office and importance, when Sandy cut the corner and I, chain extended, swept around behind him. The chain caught the sheriff across the middle and seated him suddenly on the sidewalk.

This was a man who dealt regularly with the criminal class and could speak their language. His expressions of discomfort were horrendous. I was, among other things, firmly advised to shorten the chain to avoid those sweeping corners. All this while he remained seated on the walk and Sandy, always replete with irrepressible affection, licked his face to a nicety. This seemed to soften the sheriff, both literally and emotionally, so all ended reasonably well.

Sandy could also be hooked up to my wooden-sided wagon and make great speed around the neighborhood, dirt roads and all. Later, when I bought my $5 bike, Sandy, hitched by a chain to the handle bars provided its major power.

Most comforting was his happy night station at the foot of my bed against constant parental objection. Our house was heated by a living room stove and a kitchen stove, so not much heat achieved the attic rooms. No matter, toes under a dog are a source of comfort and warmth.

That is but one side of the story. Sandy loved other people too, and would greet them with great affection. Tall enough to leap at anyone he thought worth his attention, he would place both paws on the shoulders of his victim and give any face a thorough, joyous licking.

Raymond Birch, our strong and sturdy postman, received this joyous attention without complaint. In fact, he seemed to look forward to Sandy's greetings. But frailer ladies passing by, and assaulted in the same fashion, often nearly bowled over, chose to file frequent complaints.

After some time, it came to pass that my parents, in union, decided that Sandy was too large and too hungry for our yard and should be sent to a farm or some equivalent acreage where he could be free to roam and run. This was an adult point of view, certainly not mine.

It came to pass that Mr. and Mrs. LeBroke owned a nearby farm which was frequently invaded by munching deer. Sandy, they claimed, would be a welcome blessing. So, it fell upon me one day, under parental command, to hook Sandy to my bike and ride to the LeBroke's town home and chain him to the handle of their garage door and ride away, the good dog straining mightily at his chain and barking his heart out. I never saw him again. I grieved silently for a very long time.

I would lie if I did not admit to a resulting coldness and distrust settling deep inside and never since eased or altered.

This internal and eternal sentiment has nothing to do with thought or wisdom, or anything to do with maturity and time. Parting with Sandy was intellectually necessary I know, since I can reason. But it was also emotionally devastating. I know that because I can feel it to this very day. There are times, I believe, when logic and convenience must be set aside. Some forced separations are unforgivable and there is no closure!

Railroad Trips

I made one railroad trip with Dad on the 'Mina Run' or, as he called it in those earlier prejudiced days, 'The Squaw Train.' To keep working, some of the younger railroad men had to accept assignments on the 'narrow gauge runs' which had to do with a long spur line to the town of Mina (suitably named for its mining operations) at the southern part of Nevada, or into the High Sierras for work on the logging trains, also narrow gauge.

The Mina run had a 'mixed train.' That is, there were one or two passenger cars (as need be) mostly freight cars, and that wonderful place called a caboose.

On my journey to Mina with Dad, I chose the caboose for most of the trip. It had a small balcony at the back end where you could stand and watch the tracks grow ever closer to one another as they vanished over the fading horizon. Or you could climb up a small ladder to a square cupola at the top of the caboose and see in any direction. There were two padded seats up there, not entirely unlike my window seat.

The caboose contained a large, black, pot-bellied stove with a flat top for cooking or making coffee. It had a pair of unfolding bunks lower down on which one could sleep. There was a folding table you could raise from against one wall to eat on. All in all, if a bit bouncy, it was a happy way to travel.

From time to time, when the train made a station stop I could, if I wanted, move into one of the passenger cars and spend some time there. I did that rarely on the trip, preferring my private adventures and dominion over the caboose.

While we were in Mina we ate at the same restaurant every day. The waitress, named Mamie, and Dad seemed to enjoy each other's company enormously. I gathered from the conversations and their tone that they knew each other very well and from several different places. I thought nothing of it until, on our way home, Dad closed his left eye and raised his right eyebrow, which he did when there was something serious he wished me consider, and said, 'I'd prefer you didn't mention Mamie to your mother. I never did.

My second railroad trip was made years later to San Francisco on an overnight sleeper to visit my Aunt in Oakland and my sister in San Francisco where she was attending the Franklin Hospital School of Nursing. Those were San Francisco's days of clanging street cars and the 'Key' system.

Necessities

If your mother happened to be British, and you happened to be sent to school, you were put into short pants with knee socks. This in the United States, in a railroad and farm community where most of the boys wore overalls or cords or levis — long pants all — is to ask for trouble, the more particularly when you have skipped kindergarten and are, as a result, the dwarf in the class.

After I had been tormented a while, Billy Zenclusen, a sturdy farm boy, by far the largest fellow in the second grade, suggested that if I helped him with his school work — and he needed all the help he could get — he would see to my physical safety when at school.

I helped him with his classes and he, a dutiful fellow, took care of the matter of my past, present, or future tormenters, even after I had revolted in the third grade and refused to go to school until provided with suitable long pants. Mother was upset. Dad was sympathetic and firm. We went to the Toggery and I got my long cords.

Billy stayed with his sense of bodyguard duties even through our high school years, though his services were no longer actually required.

It was no longer necessary, after grammar school, for me to assist him very often with his homework. By then I was editor of the high school newspaper. But Billy had earned the privilege of being able to hide under my work table in the back Journalism room, for his needed afternoon naps.

I should mention cords, the pants of our school careers. They were of a dark tan with heavily ribbed cloth and were not intended, as far as we were concerned, to ever see the inside of a washing machine. The name of the game was to allow them to gather dirt and ink-written notes from others until, at the end of the day, when you took them off, they could stand in your room on their own.

Unfortunately, mothers had a tendency, at disgraceful moments, to throw them into the washing machine. The colors were not fast, and eventually one's cords turned white — disgraceful. A new pair had to be acquired shortly thereafter.

Levis, most often worn by the ranch kids, were the alternative to cords, or rarely, as in the case of Billy Zenclusen or Dean McNeilly, overalls were de rigor.

Home and Library

There were no sidewalks and no paved streets in our immediate neighborhood. The walkways in the front and back yards of our new home were one-by-twelve-inch planks embedded in the grass. I learned to roller skate on those boards.

The house had certain features that I thought amazing. In the pantry there was a rope and pulley mechanism that lowered a small screened box, with a latching door in it, down through the floor into a very deep pit in the ground under the house. It was called a 'cooler.' Mother would put the milk and butter in the cage and turn a crank to lower the screened container down, down, down out of sight into the cooler regions. When we later got an ice box Dad tore out the cooler system.

The flush toilet in the only bathroom was also fascinating. There was a walnut box way up high near the ceiling and an exterior pipe extending down to the toilet. A chain with a round wooden knob at the end hung from the box. To flush the toilet, you reached up a little and pulled the chain and water came cascading down the pipe with a satisfactory rush, and thus the toilet flushed.

As a result, I have an accurate notion of what we mean when we tell someone to lay off or we will 'pull his chain.' That's not a common way to say 'back off' anymore, since technology has a habit of altering language.

In the backyard we had a small tin-roofed lean-to shed called a 'tool shed.' Beside it was a massive barn-like older building which was the wood and coal shed.

When I joined the Boy Scouts my dad said he would move his tools into a section of the wood shed and I could clean out and use the tool shed for a meeting room for the Boy Scouts.

I cleaned and painted the inside of the shed and Dad made benches for us to sit on. The shed had a broad wooden workbench and two windows, one above the workbench and the other that faced out into the alley. The workbench was perfect for working on Merit Badge items. I stayed in the Scouts until I made Life Scout. But I never continued on to Eagle Scout — high school had other interests such as my getting to be editor of the school paper called 'The Streamliner,' which I eventually achieved.

We also had a root cellar with hinged wooden doors. It was filled with clean sand and it was in the sand that I buried most of the root products of the vegetable garden to be dug out during the middle of the winter. Items there remained remarkably preserved.

Mr. Carnegie gave Sparks a library — a nice little brick building. Our library was on the second floor reached by a dual set of outdoor steps on the west and on the east meeting at a landing on the top. Below these horizontal steps and constituting a second front door, there were rented law offices.

When you reached the library entrance on the second floor, you turned right for the children and young adult section and left for the adult section. Each had a fairly large reading room with the stacks to the rear.

All stacks were open for browsing, but Mrs. Spencer, the librarian, or Mrs. Devine, her assistant, kept a watchful eye that we did not cross in front of the main desk into an 'inappropriate' section. Children were always firmly but gently taught their place in those days.

The library was my favorite reading spot next to my window seat, no doubt of that. Either on the way to, or on the way home, from church, I would stop in at the library and read the Sunday funnies in the San Francisco Examiner or the San Francisco Chronicle. For this I had to receive permission (always granted) to cross over to the adult section of the library. Later, when I was a junior in high school, I was granted the right to enter the adult section without special permission.

Before then, I would also pick up the latest Oz book whenever available. They seemed to come out about once a year, stretching from Baum's original story in 1900, up through 1939.

L. Frank Baum wrote the first fourteen Oz books. Ruth Plumly Thompson took over in 1921 and wrote nineteen more. The illustrator, who followed after the original book artist, John R. Neill, wrote three much less successful follow-ups. Jack Snow wrote two. Rachel R. Cosgrove wrote one, and Eloise Jarvis McGraw & Lauren McGraw Wagner wrote the final book.

Mr. Baum's tales were whimsical and often inconsistent. Too, he did not understand about children, maybe because he was male. Ruth Plumly Thompson did.

And what was the problem? Intelligent children do not believe in silly magic. It is not possible, even though the author says it is so, to talk out of your ear. It is not possible for a tree to pull up its roots and walk, magic notwithstanding. A turnstile can grab you but cannot free itself from its cement base. If, in your magic land, as Baum would have it, east is west and west is east, then south ought to be north and north should be south. But Mr. Baum forgot that and created a lot of confusion. Children have a sharp eye for any inconsistency.

Mrs. Thompson understood that for children, magic must have credibility, and children have a keen eye for contradiction. A tree could only reach out and grab you with its branches, or hurl its apples at you if it chose.

A horse could have telescopic legs and be, on choice, a highboy or a lowboy. That is permissible. It is a truly subtle business. The later authors missed that and many other points. I know these things because I'm an official Oztorian, and I have the certificate somewhere around to prove it signed by H.M. Wogglebug T.E. himself.

It was H.M. Wogglebug T.E. who created my ambition to be a professor. Originally, a small bug, he lived on the fireside hearth of a college professor. The professor was of a habit of reading aloud and, preparing his lectures, also practicing them aloud too. Hence, the Wogglebug became T.E. (thoroughly educated).

It was the professor's habit to study the Wogglebug under a magnifying glass until, highly magnified, the Wogglebug reached a full six feet in height. Hence H.M. Wogglebug T.E., the founder of the University of Oz wherein all knowledge lessons were dealt with by simply taking a proper History, Astronomy, Physics or Literature pill while the main activity was athletics — which is where, given the alumni, most universities would readily go if they only had the pills prepared by Professor Wogglebug.

I recall (more on that later) being horrified when Tip turned into Ozma of Oz. That was before Denmark or 'gay' meant anything other than playful and happy. It seemed to me, at the time, that no boy, magic or not, would ever permit himself the infinite disaster of being turned into a girl.

I had two sisters, and knew something about the complexities of their existence and appearances verses my simple splash of water and quick comb of hair and out into the world. I mean, who would choose all that makeup and hair-doing and girdles and stocking seams etc. etc. etc.? Good grief, girls did not get to discard their shoes very often during the summer, and if they went skinny dipping, I never heard of it!

I think Mr. Baum and Mrs. Thompson should be given credit by women in no small way. Dorothy, and her friend Trot, had guts. They did not scream or faint, they dealt with troubles and adventures as they came along. They had a lot of straightforward common sense that frequently paid off. The gnome king was no trivial foe, you know. They were, to be blunt, the kind of girls that, if one had to hang out with girls, one would prefer to hang out with.

Later, I did sneak a reading, from time to time, of my older sister's Nancy Drew mystery stories. Nancy, with her convertible, and guts, and gal friends seemed to me to be okay!

Forgive me, modern librarians, but if you still oppose the Oz books, you are idiots! It was in those works that I learned that courage and common sense were not confined to boys.

Bicycles

Bicycles were hard to come by during the Great Depression — at least for most of us. But Dad did visit the junk yard, found an old discarded bike frame, and some wheels, and patiently assembled a rather crude bicycle for me. He spent a lot of time straightening out the wheels by virtue of a special tool for tightening spokes — that much I remember clearly.

For me the bike provided the difficulty of being too large a frame, sans fenders, and somewhat rusty overall. With no fenders you got wet front and back during stormy weather. But it was on that ungainly instrument I learned to ride.

I regret that I did not really appreciate Dad's work as much as I should have, after I got over the initial excitement. But I did, a couple of years later, with $5 of my lawn-mowing money, manage to buy Howard Owens's old bicycle — a smaller more manageable size, a single color, and equipped with fenders, a light, and other luxuries.

The 'new' bike lasted me through my high school years, though by that time it was likely to be thought a bit too small.

Mostly I remember pedaling anywhere it was necessary to go (Reno included) and never suffering from tired legs or any noticeable sign of fatigue. We had PE classes, to be sure, but the fact of the matter is that we really did not need them.

Facilities and Luxuries

Early 1933 was the year we got our first radio, which was a round-topped table model placed on the piano because that was close to one of the two wall plugs my dad had wired into the living room.

When we first moved into one house, the electrical lights extended from a twisted yellow cord in the ceiling and had a single bulb and an open (upside down) flower shaped crystal shade. We had several kerosene lamps in reserve because the Sparks electrical power was sporadic. I had the chore, because my hands were small, of taking a soft scrap of cloth and cleaning the glass chimneys of the lamps when they got smoked.

I'm certain of the time when we got our radio because the first thing we listened to, in our 'permanent' home, as a family, was President Franklin D. Roosevelt's inaugural address.

Around this time, Dad added a glassed-in back porch made up of curved windows from junked old railroad passenger cars. A few years later, when the dime store moved — I worked there, stocking shelves and sweeping and oiling the wooden floors — and all their glass shelf dividers became mere scrap, I brought a lot of them home and my dad bought metal brackets to attach them at the bottom of the double row of windows thus providing my mother with many shelves for her plants.

It was a pleasant, sunny, greenery filled room that always, even in the winter, smelled of blooming flowers.

We had a wood/coal stove in the living room and a wood/coal stove in the kitchen. My job was to shake out the ashes each morning and carry them out and spread them in our vegetable garden area to be later spaded under to enrich the soil. Then I went to the wood shed and chopped mill blocks for kindling and filled two coal scuttles, one for each stove. Then I would crumple up old pages from the Reno Evening Gazette, place the finer kindling over it with a larger block or two above and light the fire with big wooden matches taken from a match box attached to the wall near the stove. When the two fires got going well, I added more blocks and pieces of coal. In due course, we had that localized comfort that only a wood fire can bring.

A big bare water tank sat in the corner of the kitchen and beside it a painted wood box my dad had built. During winter days my job was to be sure the wood box was filled, morning and evening, and the two scuttles filled with coal likewise.

Bare pipes ran from the water tank to the firebox of the kitchen stove. The water tank eventually exuded its own warmth and the best place to read or sit was on top of the wood box sandwiching oneself between the stove and the water heater — very comfortable, even on the coldest days when the distant corners of every room were somewhat chilly. I spent a lot of time there.

Refrigerators were rare, expensive and somewhat experimental. We relied on an ice box, and it fell upon me to keep the basin at the bottom, behind a wooden flap, drained of water. We toasted our bread on top of the stove, held slightly above the hot surface by what looked like a wire, square, double-sided tennis racket which opened up and clamped the bread inside.

My mother used sad irons that were heated on the right side of the stove, so the ironing board was nearby — not too pleasant, I would imagine, during the summer months. Perhaps that is how they came to be called 'sad' irons.

Mother did the laundry in the bathtub with a brass scrub board. One of the sounds I can still remember is the sound of her wedding ring sometimes rasping down the brass ridges on the board. She wrung out the clothes by hand and hung them out in the yard (any season) on three clothes lines that stretched from the back stoop to the wood shed.

One of my minor chores was to follow Mother when she un-clipped the clothes and stuffed them into my arms. I remember how fresh they always smelled. She had an apron with a pocket into which she dropped the recovered clothes pins.

My principal job for my father, who was forever rebuilding the house, was to hold things steady.

Thus, I learned electric wiring, carpentry, skills with a paint brush and plumbing, all of which have saved me, I would guess, at least half my salary every year of my working life. Material costs have been my only problem through the years.

We also had flower gardens and a huge vegetable garden, and I have a reasonably green thumb as a result.

Since practically everyone in Sparks was connected with the Southern Pacific Railroad one way or another, the Great Depression hit everyone in a similar fashion and we had little to compare in the way of the rich and the poor.

I think, for those of us who were young, the great gift was the necessity of making our own toys and amusements. We learned a special kind of creativity and independence which seldom seems to be forced upon the young today.

One of the oddities of the Depression was the constant availability, in our house, of vegetables and fresh fruits, though meat was scarce. We grew most of our own vegetables which were 'put by' (canned) by Mother for the winter months.

The railroad men, under the guidance of the Agriculture Act were supposed to take crates of vegetables and fresh fruits and dump them in the Nevada desert. They did just that, after picking the best crates for themselves and dumping the others within walking distance of those linear little towns made up of converted box cars which stretched along the rails in the Nevada desert and were occupied by the families of the section hands.

There were many hungry children about. To waste the food struck the railroad men as absurd. They dumped as ordered, but in places of their own selection.

From time to time, my dad would take my wagon to work. He always returned with a crate of apples, or apricots, or pears or oranges. We had more fine fresh fruit then than ever since. Fresh pears were always exciting. Around Christmas we were fairly buried in Tangerines.

Cars

Even though we never owned a car, I naturally had an affinity for them, collecting toy versions whenever it was possible and well aware of the models and makes moving around our local highways and byways at the time.

My sisters went along happily with their dolls (paper and china) and any number of other non-mechanical and frilly doings, unconcerned and unsympathetic with any of my mechanical interests.

Much later, I learned to drive in the 1932 Chevrolet two-door sedan of a high school friend. It had, as I recall, a composition roof which needed sealing treatment from time to time. It was not until 1935 that the all-steel auto top hit our neighborhood.

Roadsters with rumble seats were our dream cars, or, really going into fantasy, Tom Mix's Duesenberg, or the famous Cord which introduced front-wheel drive.

I was most familiar with the more mundane cars of the period which included a 1934 Ford V-8. Its doors opened from center hinges, which meant the back doors were much like those of our modern cars, but the front doors were the reverse, and there were occasional reports of them being opened in transit and being torn off by the wind and the luckless opener hurled out onto the street or highway. The V-8 engine, capable of rapid acceleration, was much admired in my set. The model was later featured in the movie 'Bonnie and Clyde.'

It was a big event on the block, among the younger lads, when Mr. Jones turned in his big, square, 1928 Dodge, with its reverse gearshift, for a 1936, all steel, streamlined, Plymouth. It was the wonder of the block and in his pride he took several of us on drives around the immediate area.

A couple of my friends in high school had stripped-down old Model 'T' Fords and turned them into primitive versions of our modern dune buggies. We did a lot of adventuring in the desert areas surrounding Sparks and Reno, particularly in the stretch of desert between Sparks and Pyramid Lake.

We visited the highway only on occasion. When we encountered a hill too steep to drive up — the Model 'T' had a gravity feed and not a fuel pump — we simply turned the 'T' around and backed up the hill.

Some of the high school fellows had Model 'A' Fords and one lucky fellow had a Model 'B.' They would not meet safety muster now, as the gas tank was integrated into the dashboard and replete with a bubble gauge that told you, eye to eye, how much fuel you had.

The wealthy Bovee D. drove a 1940 Oldsmobile with a new wonder, an automatic transmission. The P. sisters (also wealthy) drove a 1940 DeSoto with some equal magic called 'fluid drive.' Most everyone else made do with gearshifts which had by1940 been moved up from the floor to the steering column.

Our algebra teacher, Miss Stone drove a Nash which had some odd kind of push button gearshift which was also a sensation. Too, it was equipped with another first, an air conditioner.

I took my official high school driving lessons in a 1940, dark green Ford coupe with the shift on the steering column. Happily, to take the lessons, it didn't matter whether we owned a car or not.

One of our neighbors owned an ancient Essex which was in mint condition. This, due to the fact that, as far as we knew, he took it out of the garage each Saturday, washed and waxed it, and then put it back inside. No one ever reported having seen him actually drive the car off the property. Perhaps ownership was sufficient?

Of the high school crowd, William V. was the only fellow who had a convertible. It proved fatal. He was racing amidst the trees in Idlewild Park one afternoon when he flipped the car and was decapitated. The story was that his head rolled along and destroyed the demeanor of a nearby picnicking family. The latter part of the news could, of course, have been apocryphal.

No counselors showed up at Sparks High. We were simply informed by the teachers, if asked, that speed and stupidity were often fatal at any age and, if we had any sense and wished to stay alive, we would learn a lesson and drive carefully.

Mining with Mr. Ball

I had a grammar school friend named Donald Ball. I do not know what his father did except that he was one of those fellows who constantly sought his fortune in spare-time gold mining.

On those occasions when Mr. Ball decided to make a trip to his own mine along the Walker River, Donald insisted I go along. We were stuffed into the back seat of Mr. Ball's Reo automobile along with bedding, pillows, and other necessary camping gear.

Mr. Ball was a chain smoker and a rather neurotic driver, perhaps merely inexperienced. We were instructed to be very quiet and not distract Mr. Ball when he was driving and chain smoking.

When we arrived at our destination, an old and badly neglected cabin on one side of the river, Mrs. Ball spent a good while cleaning out the place, and arranging food and bedding. We happily accompanied Mr. Ball to his mine shaft, though we were forbidden to enter it.

We crossed the river on a small metal box hanging beneath a metal cable that stretched across the river. We had to make the trips individually and both of us were advised to keep a careful watch on our fingers as we reached for the cable and pulled the cart along to the other side of the river.

The Walker River was a swift-moving stream. Sometimes we crossed the river by holding on to Mr. Ball's hand as he worked his way through the rapids, using his big mining pick to keep on his feet. This too was great sport. While crossing the stream we would almost be swept downstream in a near horizontal position with only Mr. Ball's strong grasp to keep us from floating away.

Most of our eating was outside the cabin. Mr. Ball had erected what we would, these days, call a stone BBQ topped with a metal grill. It was there are main meals were prepared.

Mr. Ball, however tense he might have been as a motorist, was otherwise relaxed and, when we were gathered around the fire as the sun set, he told wonderful ghost stories about old mines and old miners who haunted abandoned mine shafts and hoarded gold.

Mr. Ball did actually have gold in his mine. And, at the end of a few days mining, as we returned home, he would announce his satisfaction.

'Near a hundred fifty dollars this time,' he would report to Mrs. Ball. That may not seem like much money in these inflationary days, but in the 1930s it was a worthwhile income, particularly for a hobby.

I'm not certain how many trips I made to the Walker River mine with Donald and his family. Certainly we made more than one or two, as I have very clear memories of the cabin and the tram car over the river and, as I remember, became quite skillful about crossing the river without running the pulley over my fingers.

Childhood's End

I cannot find many people who can remember the date and time of their childhood's end. In my own case, I can give you the exact date and the exact time — December 24, 1938 at 11:45 p.m. It had nothing to do with budding puberty (I was a bit slow about that matter). It had to do with Christmas.

I cannot speak for other households, but at our house Dad put up the tree, which he had been preserving in the cold outside weather for a week or more, on Christmas Eve. During that time he bored a few holes and added a few branches here and there from a spare tree he always got cheap because it was misshapen. This made the indoor tree as symmetric as possible.

Then, because Santa Claus knew nothing of electrical matters (save in toys), Dad patiently mounted the tree in a wooden stand and put on the tree lights. We could watch that performance before going off to bed.

The lights were those larger, old-fashioned bulbs, with the tree protected from the direct heat by 'reflectors' — colorful leafed-foil shields that accentuated the glitter of the bulbs. But it was Santa Claus who decorated the tree, and spread the presents around while we were slumbering in our beds, or wishing we could.

My two sisters (one older by three years and one younger by five) and I would naturally rise at some ungodly hour Christmas morning in great excitement — usually around five thirty or six, and trot downstairs, at which point Dad would get out of bed and build a fire in both stoves (though the curtains were drawn in the doorway between the kitchen and the living room) and make breakfast.

For us, waiting for Mother to appear, and to be required to eat hot cereal before the curtains would be parted, was an almost unendurable agony.

But the curtains were eventually drawn and we rushed into the room lit only by the glorious fire of the Christmas lights and the awesomely glittering bulbs, and tinsel, and icicles, of the tree, around the base of which Santa had left his presents, and Mother our other gifts, all very magnificently wrapped in colored paper with glittering bows.

Mostly Santa's main presents were not wrapped — one time, an ivory radio (from Sears) for my older sister, and a brown radio (from Wards) for me, and a specially requested doll awaited my younger sister.

But back to childhood's departure: I turned thirteen (November 21, 1938) and so, for Christmas had asked for a single-shot 22 rifle, from 'Santa Claus' (still kept alive out of respect for my younger sister who, though she had her suspicions, wasn't yet certain).

It was a very busy time at the Sprouse-Reitz five-and-ten-cent store, so on Christmas Eve we stayed open until eight and I, manning one of the cash registers, did not get around to my normal stocking and swamping chores until I had cleared the registers, put the money in the canvas bag and hidden it in the stockroom. Even the manager (Brian Laveaga) did not know where the cash was hidden until I appeared each morning at 7:30 to refill the registers. It was a marvelous trust on his part and I never forgot it.

I arrived home very late Christmas Eve and came in the front way. Mother and Dad already had gone to bed. One dim lamp burned in the living room that I might find my way. The Christmas tree was unlit, but fully decorated. The presents from Santa, including my 22-rifle, were laid out around the base of the tree along with the family presents. I surveyed (but did not touch) my rifle, nodded my head in satisfaction and went to bed for a night's undisturbed rest, confident of the future.

Childhood's end came then, with just a touch of sorrow at maturity and the loss of the glowing expectations which awaited my younger sister. Sometimes it is sad to have passed one of the pleasant morning surprises of childhood and joined the jaded 'adult' world. But, there also came a certain sense of pride and satisfaction with 'being in the know.'

Cooking

Some of the other great joys of childhood rest on unsullied senses. Devoid of the expectations of experience, children do not look *to* see, they look *and* see. This is why they are very difficult audiences for slight-of-hand artists. They watch with tenacious care and cannot be verbally distracted.

Unsullied taste is one of the greatest of childhood gifts. Or perhaps I cared more than the ordinary because, if there was one great truth in our household, it was that my mother could not cook very well. Over the years, my dad, my sisters and I learned the basic kitchen arts in self defense.

My grandfather (James Fraser) was Chief Game Keeper to Lord Lovat. He only surrendered his rule of the hunting lodge (a huge affair replete with many servants and abutting Loch Ness with the Tor castle Keep always visible on the horizon in all its magnificently bleak decay) when Lord Lovat brought a hunting party to the lodge, two or three times a year at most. Then, and only then, the Frasers ate below in the kitchen — my mother's only contact with the place. One does not learn from infrequent visitation.

As a child, I quickly discovered there were ladies in the neighborhood who could cook, and a visit was always rewarding. Mrs. Ball, two blocks away, baked fresh bread two or three times a week. She also made apple butter and kept it in cool crocks. A friendly visit to Mrs. Ball's on Tuesdays and Fridays, when she did her baking, almost always resulted in a large slab of warm fresh bread topped with a thick layer of apple butter. Our bread was 'Wonder' and came from the grocery store. Any apple butter we had arrived in a jar.

I have already mentioned Mrs. Williams and her parrot and her way of always having on hand varieties of freshly made cookies. The parrot loved cookies. I loved cookies too. We were conspiratorial in our association.

Mrs. Lightfoot made candies, and had the build to prove the constant sampling of her own wares. In particular, she made fudge and divinity (the whiter fluffier candy). I could skip the divinity, but never the large chunks of dark chocolate fudge riddled with walnuts.

At Halloween, children were known to walk the length of the town in order not to do without Mrs. Lightfoot's homemade handouts. It paid to be friendly with Mrs. L., because that meant a great box of various candies would be your Christmas gift. The peanut brittle still lives in memory. I've searched for a match for years and never found one.

One of our neighbors, Mr. Thorsen, was a professional baker. During the depression, to supplement his income, he created gloriously tiered wedding cakes at home. They were always latticed with white sugar creations. A visit there often uncovered a not-quite-empty frosting bowl to be scraped to a gleam with busy fingers. A well-frosted, lickable digit is a childhood memory not to be lightly dismissed.

This is not to say my mother did not eventually learn to cook certain things reasonably well: the Christmas and Thanksgiving turkeys, a baked ham, roast beef and Yorkshire pudding and a leg of lamb.

First time around — acceptable, sometimes even grand. But after that, the frying pan — ad lib and eternal — warming over items the deadliest way. Have you ever had fried mashed potatoes? If not, skip the experience. You would also do well to avoid reheated Brussels sprouts. Ugh!

It always seemed to me that the art of cooking is the art of dealing inventively and tastefully with leftovers. Turkey hash (fried), lamb hash (also fried) and beef hash (again fried), all without any other accouterments, are, to be kind, nothing more than grim sustenance!

Dad made coffee. Mother made tea. My older sister made the cakes. My dad made pies with crusts suitable for soling shoes. He could, though, make tasty fudge — stored in large jars for the holiday season. When home, he always made breakfast. Dry cereals triumphed when he was away on the railroad.

I made three-decker, toasted sandwiches of the 'club' variety — often for an evening snack when Mrs. Henry from across the street visited of an evening. Mrs. Henry was very complimentary of my three-decker sandwiches.

From time to time, Dad on the road and my sisters off on some occasion or other, Mother would say. 'Go get hamburgers and I'll make tea.'

The Circus

Between Sparks and Reno existed the empty stretch I've mentioned as Coney Island.

One day Dad announced that the giant Ringling Brothers circus was actually coming to Reno and would be set up in Coney Island, a reasonable walk from our house.

It was a 'once in a lifetime affair,' Dad noted and saved his money. I think the sum he paid for the tickets for the family to see the circus was an awesome $7. That was no small change at the time.

The circus parade was to begin at the east end of Sparks and go west to Reno. It would pass but one block north of our house. Then, he noted, we could later simply walk over to see the circus itself.

It was my first sight of elephants and my first sight of clowns. Mostly I remember the clowns were riding the elephants and doing stunts on their backs. I also remember a carillon wagon, pulled by horses making magic music with their jingling bells. I'd never heard sounds like that before. A little later in the parade was the calliope, a marvelously loud and colorful wagon drawn by four jeweled and bedecked horses on whose backs rode the trapeze artists clad in costumes of gold.

And what can I recall of the circus itself? A memory of a tiny little car out of which some fifteen or more clowns appeared remains a highlight. I was awed that so many people could stuff so small a space. And the trapeze act — truly awesome. I don't recall a net. And another treat I'd never dreamed of — cotton candy — a great pink cloud of sticky sweet stuff that disappeared into your mouth with almost no effort. One touched the sugary cloud with one's lips and just inhaled. Certainly I should mention the Cracker Jack box with its little toy surprise. Oh glorious event!

On the way home, my mother fretted about the cost of it all and my dad's extravagance. Dad insisted it was worth it. The Ringling Brothers circus, he said, was not likely to ever come our way again. It was for my sisters and me he insisted, and well worth the cost, and hadn't mother enjoyed herself? Well yes, as a matter of fact she had, mostly because the costumes were so clean and beautifully kept. We each had our priorities.

Depression 'Drifters'

An enormous number of able-bodied young men were cast adrift in the United States during the Great Depression. Their movement plagued the railroads and their men who sometimes took savage action against the young 'hobos' and 'drifters.' Exceptions were places like Sparks where the railroader were of a more sympathetic bent.

I can remember grubby, tired, worn, young men coming up the back alley, through the gate and knocking on our door to ask if there was any work they could do for something to eat. They made no attempt to enter the house, which would have been a simple matter with doors that were never locked and my mother alone much of the time.

I asked my mother why they always came in the back way. She said, 'because they are young and strong and proud and can't get work. It makes them ashamed, though surely, in these pinching times, they need not be.'

They came, knocked on the back door and asked if there was any work. Usually, my mother told them she had nothing for them to do, which I resented because I thought she might well pass on the chores of loading the coal scuttles or chopping a large helping of mill blocks — but she would make them a sandwich. Somehow we always had something or other available — and, in the meanwhile, they were to go to the wood shed, where there was a large washtub, take the hose and have a bath and wash their clothes. She accompanied these instructions with a Naptha soap bar and a clean towel.

When they had finished bathing and had washed their clothes, I would appear with the sandwich and milk, if available, and would hang their wet clothes on the line. In Nevada, things dried out very rapidly. When their clothes were dry, I would give them back and they could be on their way.

These tired fellows were always gracious in their thanks. They always emptied and hung up the tub and gave me the soap to return. They always looked better when they left than when they arrived because, they were now clean and fresh and, if severely tattered on arrival, my mother sometimes gifted them with a pair of my father's old overalls.

The late Eric Sevareid, always spoke well of Sparks, Nevada as contrasted with conditions faced by young itinerants in the Midwest and particularly Wyoming, since he was one of them. I would like to believe that one day he came down our alley, through our back gate, knocked on our back door, was given a ham sandwich or some other item of food by my mother and availed himself of our washtub and soap. That was not likely, but it was a cheerful thought.

From time to time, during the Great Depression, the Southern Pacific railroad came to a near halt. Accordingly, to keep us going, my dad worked for the WPA or PWA (I never could tell which was which) involving such work as mending streets, installing sewer lines, weeding vacant lots and the like. He suggested to me and my two sisters that, if we saw him involved in such labor, we could pretend we did not know him. This we did not understand and, when we did see him weeding some vacant lot or other, happily waved his way.

In large part his shame was due to the virulent screams of the Republicans of the time about 'making work,' and 'boondoggling,' 'coddling,' and 'wasted' money. One can only hope they are burning or starving is some special hell somewhere.

It was hardly so to us as children, because those activities were what kept us from literally starving to death, along with the tinned beef and other items coming from the Federal Government and which my father hid under the stairs until needed. Looking back, his pride was foolish, but it was admirable.

Sleds

It was during 1937 that the U. S. weather turned foul. In the summer most of the Midwestern soil was in the air, moving south and making deserts. In Nevada, during the winter, it was colder than usual. We had, just before Christmas, one of those dreamed of thrills — Sparks and Reno were under no less than three feet of snow, with flakes still falling. And, by a stroke of luck, we had asked for sleds for Christmas.

It was the Depression, so our new sleds were small and short and did not have flexible runners for steering. You headed downhill and the sled went where it wanted to go. I learned, lying on the sled, to drag one foot or the other behind, and could actually change my direction. My sisters let things go, though they did, with an eye on obstacles, try to point their sleds in a safe direction. My challenge was to head in the direction of disaster and see if I could steer my way out of it. I did not always succeed.

With so much snow underfoot, one could build huge snowmen. My trick was to begin my snowman by rolling a snow ball at the back of the property (some 150 feet deep) and then, weaving my way toward the street, resulting in an enormous size, nearly my own height.

Getting the snowman's smaller middle and his head on presented something of a problem. I used planks. I leveled the top of the snowman's base, then braced a plank against him and (with a good deal of slippage) managed to roll his middle up the plank, level that top in turn, shift the plank to a steeper plane and roll his head (not so difficult to handle) into place.

We had lots of pea coal for eyes and lips, and I dug a carrot out of the root cellar for his nose. My dad's old straw hat (called a 'boater') topped all, and Mother gave me an old woolen scarf for his neck. He was a splendid fellow. I had also received (things were a little better financially) a Kodak Brownie (box) camera. They cost $1. The camera took wonderful pictures — point and shoot.

The snowman was photographed and later put into my scrapbook which I kept from childhood through high school graduation. It vanished between the time I went off to WWII and my return, along with my comic book collection (the first Batman, Superman, Green Hornet etc.). My

Mother knew it not, but she threw away a future fortune.

The Jack's Carnival

Every spring, Sparks held the 'Jack's Carnival.' I don't know who Jack was or what he did, but the carnival was fun. All along the park, that stretched, as I've mentioned, from the western edge of Sparks to its eastern edge fading into the desert, booths were set up. They served fine foods of various kinds, candies, games etc. We also had a Jack's Carnival parade in which all the young people participated. We met, class by class, grade by grade, at our respective schools — arriving in costume. The teachers kept us organized. The high school shop class made floats, as did some of the more prosperous businessmen. After the parade, we broke ranks and were turned loose at the carnival which lasted until just before sunset.

From a youngster's point of view, it was a wonderful institution. The park also had a circular, roofed, band stand with a nice white railing. The high school band played throughout the day with breaks for sustenance and other entertainments.

There were, as you might expect, prizes for the best costumed classes, prizes for especially ingenious individual costumes, prizes for the various athletic games played at the park, and, would you believe it, prizes for the best student orations about the affair, which I won three times.

The winner presented his essay to the public, from the band stand, while the band took a break.

There was always some wise ass of the high-school type, who came wearing the briefest possible diaper. He was usually sent directly home to put on his pants by the local sheriff. The most popular costumes, it was the West, after all, were cowboys and, more colorfully, Indians. Cap pistols added appropriate sound effects. And, there were those fellows from the high-school shop class who, with great ingenuity, created cap rifles. Real weapons, and there were plenty in town, were not allowed, and no one ever seemed to be stupid enough to bring one.

Baseball was very popular for both the young and the middle-aged. Elderly people, those approaching fifty or more, sat quietly in the shade. Some brought chairs and behaved as elderly people were supposed to behave, though most of the middle-aged ladies were busy cooking up goodies in the various booths using the camp stoves of the time.

The park is long gone — invaded by the Golden Nugget originally — and followed by its relentless expansion. The Golden Nugget, with its towers and a special ramp directly from the freeway into its parking lot, has made Sparks a lot of money and provided many jobs. But the park is gone forever, and that peculiarity of a one-sided business district which got Sparks listed in various 'believe it or not books' lives no more.

The great brick roundhouse at the eastern end of Sparks is gone, lock stock and tracks. The tiny original S. P. Station is now housed on the eastern end of town. It used to be located a few blocks from our house on the western side

Bob M.

While I sometimes envied the less restricted doings at the home of my friend Don Lightfoot, I felt very sorry for my friend Bob M.

His father was an important Southern Pacific official and so they lived in the 'better' part of Sparks in one of the 'better' houses, luxurious by the standards of the time.

Bob and I were not allowed in the living room, an elegant affair with very chic furnishings. Nor were we allowed to play in the manicured back or front yards of his home. They too were off limits. We were told to go off and play in the school yard or nearby park. Bob's bedroom had a separate outside entrance, so that's the only part of his home with which I (or Bob for that matter) was familiar.

Bob was an only child and somewhat overfed. He thoroughly enjoyed visiting our house and wrestling with my big dog Sandy who had to settle for a tie more often than a victory as he was simply outweighed by Bob.

One time when Bob was visiting us, sitting in our living room, he commented to my mother, 'I really like your house, Mrs. Laurie.'

'It's not very elegant,' my mother admitted.

'No,' Bob admitted, 'but you live in it.'

When he had gone, I said, 'Poor Bob!'

'I know,' Mother allowed.

Admonitions

My mother, a well-educated woman, none-the-less had a phrase, mangled metaphorically, which she used with great frequency. She was always threatening to 'put her foot down with a firm hand.' Earlier on, not knowing about mixed metaphors, I merely assumed she was going to put her foot down on something (probably one of us) and re-enforce the pressure with the weight of a hand on one or the other of her arches.

Another admonition was, 'Don't do that, you'll break your neck!' I suppose in those days the neck was synonymous with any possible spinal injury which might paralyze. The idea of a lifetime in an 'iron long' (the crude respirator of the day) was seldom sufficient to prevent any of us from climbing up this or that structure, tree, gravel slide or other artifact, natural or manmade.

The route between Sparks and Pyramid Lake, beginning with a street appropriately named, 'Pyramid Way' was ridden with low hills in which various fellows low on funds had dug mine shafts into the hills in the hope of striking it rich. The route was a virtual rabbit warren if you knew where to leave the road and poke around.

My mother's warning was always, 'stay out of any old mines.' My dad knew better. 'If you're going to be about poking around deserted shafts,' he would say, 'use your head.' He would hand me a small screwdriver. 'Take this with you. At the entrance of the shaft, poke it into the side timbers. If it sinks in easily, more than an inch or so, stay the hell out of that shaft. Also, look at the floor of the shaft. If it's full of rubble, stay out of it. Also, check the ceiling timbers. If you see any cross-cracks, stay the hell out of there. A lot of the fellows digging those holes wouldn't know their ass from page seven about proper timbering.'

It's odd that I never asked about this famous page seven that my dad insisted so many people didn't know their own ass from, your pardon begged. There must have been something extremely important about page seven. Maybe, I thought at the time, it contained advice in some book on how to stay alive and/or unwounded? The matter remains murky to this day.

One of our more dangerous games in later years was to spy old dynamite sticks in the occasional mine shaft and from a goodly distance shoot at them with our rifles. A hit resulted in a wonderful explosion and a subsequent cave in. These activities we kept to ourselves.

We also liked to set up old bottles or cans found in the area, or old license plates, and test our marksmanship on them. Some of my friends later became Army sharpshooters, somehow or other I managed not to acquire great skill.

Another common admonition (always ignored) was not to eat at Whitey's. Whitey's was a hamburger emporium (misusing the term) which served basic hamburgers at 5 cents each, the deluxe burgers at 10 cents each and milkshakes made of ice milk of various flavors at 10 cents each (real ice cream instead of ice milk was 15 cents). Whitey's was located half a block from the high school and junior high school and did a thriving noon business.

Much more preferable, but more expensive, was the Ramos Drugstore which had its own fountain and served tasty sandwiches. Mr. Ramos (or whoever owned the store) made his own ice cream of a richness and high quality that was indisputable. But a milkshake at the Ramos Drugstore was 20 cents. A delicious sandwich could also be had (I preferred the tuna, or the egg and olive) for 25 cents. There's no question that the Ramos Drugstore was vastly superior to Whitey's, but teen taste buds are not usually that refined, particularly when quantity is reduced for the sake of quality.

It was only after I was making money working at the Sprouse-Reitz five and dime that I happily was able to venture to Ramos's for lunch.

During the Depression one famous saying from New York or other large city was, 'Hey Buddy, can you spare a dime?' In Sparks the query was more mundane. It went, 'Hey kid, gotta nickel for a cup of coffee?'

Dad's admonition was not to give a nickel inasmuch as the asker was doubtless a drinker. I cannot recall the term 'wino' being used in those days. I don't recall the price of a drink or a bottle of cheap wine or liquor then, so I can't tell you how many nickels, given away by how many kids, were required for a drunk to continue drinking.

I will not go into a host of other warnings such as, 'Don't run with anything sharp in your hands,' 'always carry your rifle pointed down,' 'never look down the barrel of a rifle, or at least pull the bolt and empty the chamber before you do,' etc. No doubt many of them would still apply today.

Ancient Treasures

Some distance northeast of Sparks a few miles lay the city dump. It was not a landfill operation. Discards were simply hauled over a narrow dirt road and were dumped, both by the city garbage trucks and individuals with pickup trucks. It was the source of much of the materiel that we used in creating our toys and other diversions.

We all had swings in our backyards, if our backyards happened to have fairly large and sturdy trees, as most back yard did. The swing consisted of a rope tied to a sturdy branch and an abandoned automobile tire, and the source of the automobile tires? Why the city dump was one, of course.

We had a fairly wide selection in the matter of used tires. Our preference was for the large, round, thin variety. These were used on most of the older cars. In the days of my youth, that would mean cars circa 1915-1930. The larger and the thinner the tires happened to be, so much the better.

Rope was a somewhat different matter. The type we wanted had to be fairly heavy and strong. Finding old rope for a swing was a cooperative enterprise. One announced a search to one's friends and playmates, and garages, and sheds were raided. The prime places were, as it turned out, barns and vacated mine shafts.

In extremis, chains could be used. These were found here and there. They were not as scarce. Various people had heavy chains in their garages, as their cars frequently failed, and chains were needed for having them towed either to a repair garage or home. Sometimes we found sections of chain in the repair garages in town. Some were given to us and, I regret to report, some were filched. Occasionally we found such a treasure at the city dump, but not often.

We built what were called 'soap box' scooters, even though they would be more accurately described as 'orange or apple-crate' scooters. These were not available at the city dump, but could be readily found behind the three grocery stores in Sparks. And the old roller-skate halves for the scooters? Why the city dump again.

Tree houses were another construction. There were two lumber yards between Reno and Sparks in the empty stretch called Coney Island. The origin of that name was never explained, but I rather think it had to do with the fact that traveling circuses and carnivals always landed there, and there was, I later discovered, a famous Coney Island in the east with such permanent fixtures. It's just a guess.

Each of the two big lumber yards had piles of scrap lumber available to anyone who wanted to pick items out of the discards. In those days, wood was cheap and the discard piles large. It was there that we made our raids for the lumber for building our tree houses.

Crosspiece steps were nailed to the tree trunk and the tree house, often a rickety affair, was built where the major branches spread out. We sometimes required a rope long enough to extend from a trapdoor down to the ground — mostly for speedy exits. The rope was replete with knots about every foot or so to make the ascent or descent easier.

My earliest tree house turned out to be something of a disaster. Instead of a wood floor, I chose to nail a piece of discarded carpeting between two branches. I did not use large enough nails, or the heads of the nails I used were too small to avoid being pulled through the carpeting. What happened was that when I stepped onto my tree house floor it promptly tore loose and wrapped itself around me. My trip to the ground was not a source of serious wounds because my travel was interfered with by several branches and major cuts and scratches avoided because I was safely and soundly cocooned in the carpet. I hit the ground hard enough to lose my breath for a while and then, pulling body and wounded soul together, decided on wooden flooring in the future.

We did not have gangs as such in Sparks. But we did have clubs. We had a sword club, a stilt club, a fishing club, a swim club, a scooter club, a skating club, and so on. The memberships changed depending on the interest, so there was something of a communicative overlap throughout. Usually, someone in any one of the clubs was a member of several of the other clubs. I was in the sword club, the stilt club, the fishing club and the scooter club. Again, membership was not a constant matter. We shifted clubs according to season, interest and age.

I almost forgot one of the most important clubs; the train club. Most of us had electric trains circa the mid-nineteen thirties or later. I had a streamliner and a large figure-eight track set. My friend Don had freight trains and what seemed to be miles of track. We would, at his house, lay track through the living room and dining room and into his bedroom and then run his trains around for hours.

His parents were somewhat more tolerant (he was an only child) than mine, so we could sometimes leave the tracks up for several days.

These days Mr. Lightfoot would be the object of much attention due to his American Indian ancestry. In those days, the matter never came up one way or the other.

Claude C., one of our train club members once got enraged at being kept out of some event or other, and took an ax and chopped up a lot of Don's and my railroad tracks. This was considered a major crime, and his parents made him work to earn money to replace the track.

Extra track, by the way, was not available in Sparks, but could be purchased from either Montgomery Wards or Sears Roebuck in Reno. And, there was also (more expensive) a hobby shop, of sorts (called a 'novelty store') in Reno. That place was the primary source of additional cars for our train sets. Again, Don had the most cars and could, therefore, put together the longest trains which required the most tracking which required the most room.

At Christmas, some of the Reno stores would feature magnificent train sets in their windows. We were fascinated with them. They were often mounted on large plywood sheets with houses, stations, trees, switches, lights, and all. We were envious, but decided it was better to have sections of track and be able to send our trains in a variety of directions. We made tunnels out of books or block sets, and sometimes I would construct bridges with my Erector set.

The setting up of the tracks was often the most fun. Taking them apart and putting them away, usually under duress was quite another matter. There was more to it than just the tracks, as we sometimes got very ambitious about our tunnels and our bridges.

I should also like to report that railroad men don't always know what they are doing — at least in the matter of electric trains.

On the Christmas Day I was playing with my new streamliner when four railroad men visited. Naturally, they wanted to play with my train. Naturally, they managed somehow to burn out the transformer.

There were apologies and one of them went out in search of a new transformer, but came back empty handed. Stores in both Sparks and Reno were closed on Christmas Day, though the gambling halls were not. A new transformer did show up the day following, however. Dad suggested I not report the incident to my friends which, quite naturally, I ignored. Five railroad men unable to properly run a toy train? That's news which ought to be bandied about, particularly amongst one's close friends.

Boy's Toys

Because tires of an earlier day had inner tubes, we had rubber guns. A rubber gun was made by carving a piece of wood with a handle and a barrel. A clothespin was placed at the butt of the handle, held by a tightly wound inner tube band such that it put added pressure on the clamping part of the clothes pin. Another inner tube band bound the innermost handle of the clothespin tightly to the gun handle. A horizontal notch (we all had pen knives or Boy Scout knives) was carved at the end of the wooden gun barrel such that a stretched inner tube section (an over-sized rubber band, if you will) would not slip off the end. One clamped one folded end of the inner tube into the re-enforced jaw of the clothespin and then stretched the inner tube band into the notch at the end of the gun barrel.

Thus one was armed for battle. Most of the rubber guns were relatively short and the velocity of the flying piece of inner tube was limited, along with any damage it might do if it hit you. But some of the fellows made thicker cuts across old inner tubes and much longer gun barrels and created a more stinging weapon. It all depended on the muscles you could bring to bear for the stretch and the physical strength of the wood from which you carved the weapon. It may have been the Great Depression, but old inner tubes were readily available behind the town's garages and service stations. Disposal of many objects was not necessary. We took care of that problem.

A less violent and more collective game was milk tops. In that early era, milk bottles were delivered to your door by a fellow called a milkman. The bottles were made of very heavy glass so they could be returned, washed and reused. The milk was sealed in with a wax treated paper circle with a tab on it — milk tops. We collected them. A challenger hurled a milk top to the ground. You hurled your milk top after. If any part of your milk top came to rest on any part of the other fellow's milk top, you collected both and were thus the winner. If you missed, your milk top awaited the next contestant along with the one you missed.

Milk, by the way, was 5¢ a quart. One of the fun things, in the winter, about bottles of milk delivered to your front screen porch was that during the wee hours of the morning, long before anyone got up, the cream would rise to the top and turn into a kind of ice cream — very rich. This was a special treat to put on oatmeal or whatever hot cereal your parents might be forcing you to eat because it 'sticks to the ribs.' We must have had very sticky ribs in those days.

In the matter of constructing the box scooters, which we made ourselves, or had older fellows help us make, you needed about a four foot long two-by-four and an old pair of clamp-on skates.

You took the front half of one skate and nailed or screwed it to the front of the two-by-four.

The front wheels of those skates were flexible and you could change direction by merely leaning in the direction you wished to go. The back half of the skate was firmly fastened to the back of the two-by-four. The skate's steel back rest also firmly attached to the stub end of the two-by-four.

The next step was to nail an orange, or pear, or apple crate to the front of your scooter. These were two-binned affairs made of wood — light but strong. The bottoms and sides were made of wide thin slats — the top, middle, and bottom solid pieces of thicker wood.

Once you had your crate attached to your wheeled two-by-four, you had merely to put two round pieces of wood in a V (the point of the V to the front) formation on the top of the scooter box — nailed or screwed. The wood handles had to extend some way back from the wooden top of the scooter crate.

Now you had your scooter — even more fun because the crate had some of the qualities of a sounding board and exaggerated the sound of the skate wheels on the sidewalks.

Our problem, during the Depression was that Sparks did not have many sidewalks save in the shopping area and in the immediate school neighborhoods. Sometime around 1936 sidewalks came our way as a result of President Roosevelt's public works projects. At last we could ride our scooters, or skate, all over town.

Dramatics

I believe it was in my junior high 7th to 9th grades that I began a career in dramatics thanks to a young lady of my acquaintance known as Fanny M.

She was an author, a playwright, a drama coach and a star (or at least always had the lead in the plays she wrote).

We staged our performances in Fanny's garage which was actually provided with a slightly raised stage (about one foot) and curtains that could be opened or closed by means of suitable ropes and pulleys. These accomplishments were due to her father.

We charged five cents for our performances and divided the loot. As I recall, we had audiences of from five to ten people and prospered.

Fanny, after high school graduation, abjured college and went off to seek her fortune in Hollywood. I regret I never discovered whether she was a success or not. But given her drive and energy I think she must have been.

About this same time, Dorothy Jones decided we ought to form a dance band. She played the piano and was probably the most musical of us. Our knowledge came from either the grammar school or junior high school band programs and was somewhat limited. Private music lessons were rare in those days.

We met about twice a week at Dorothy's house — she had the most tolerant parents and though we practiced 'Over the Rainbow' for what seemed an eternity, we had no job offers and finally disbanded.

I kept at the tenor saxophone with the junior high and high school band and orchestras.

Sex

Sex was never discussed in our household, nor was it ever discussed in the schools that I attended except in the boys' locker room.

Looking back, the information I received in the locker room was vulgar, erroneous, and downright absurd.

The one thing we could not imagine was our parents involved in any such activity. We assumed sex was our own discovery, and we could think of no valid reason to let our parents in on the matter.

We heard of the occasional inadvertent pregnancy during our high school years, but the girl in question simply vanished and was never in school again. Today's schools are, I'm told, a bit more tolerant. I don't recall the accidental fathers in question being expelled, though some did drop out to get work because of some 'shotgun' arrangements by an angry father of the girl who had been seriously inconvenienced.

The New Garage

There came the day when Dad decided the old wood shed and the old tool shed that were at the back of our property along the alley, needed to be replaced by a new building — an actual garage — though we did not own a car, nor was there any sign that we ever would. Dad did not believe in the necessity or the safety of any vehicle that did not run on rails.

The primary reason for tearing down the wood shed was that it had suffered from auto collisions over the years and was sagging badly. The collisions were from a single source, Mrs. Long, who lived across the alley from us such that her garage opened immediately across from our sheds.

Mrs. Long was an 'impact' driver. When she backed out of her garage, she judged it was time to stop when she hit one corner of our wood shed. She then made her turn and drove out of the alley. Both her bumper and our wood shed suffered accordingly.

Dad had spoken to her many times about the matter, but Mrs. Long, if she was anything beyond a bad driver, was not one to take advice. She continued her 'impact' driving relentlessly.

Eventually, thanks to years of impact, the wood shed was in a dangerous forward-sloping condition. Dad being on the 'road' most of the time, the task of tearing down both sheds fell upon me — the joyous fancy of any growing boy — life as a wrecker.

Dad was gone for but three trips on the road before I had reduced the two sheds to rubbish and had stored the contents to be saved (tools and such) under a large tarp close to the house. The remaining wood and coal remnants lay piled in the plot normally reserved for the vegetable garden. A junk man was paid to haul the debris away to the Sparks dump.

This was also the time when Dad installed a gas floor furnace in the living room and finally persuaded my mother she could indeed cook on an electric stove.

He sold the coal and the wood blocks to a couple of retired cowboys who lived in a small shack at the end of the block. They were not of the modernizing sort, still having a well and a hand pump in their front yard.

One of my minor mysteries was that they disappeared during WWII. Their shack was torn down, and by the time I got back, a small new house rested on the property — such is progress. I asked about the fate of the two cowboys, but no one seemed to know what had happened to them.

One of Dad's determinations about the new garage was that it be suitably 'Long' proof. Accordingly, he acquired three huge 12' by 12' wooden beams two of which he embedded in deep pools of concrete to frame our garage door (which was actually never opened to my recollection). They were topped by the third 12' crossbeam. 'Now she can hit the building as often as she wants,' he noted.

She did, and one could watch the inner progress of the center of her rear bumper during subsequent months. The new garage remained unmoved and indifferent to the frequent assaults.

Shop Class

There is a painted wooden policeman cut-out that resides against one of the posts that frame our entry way in San Jose. The fellow is now 70 years old and due for another thorough sanding, filling of cracks, and paint job, as has been done several times these last 20 years. My goal has been to preserve the original wood from which he was carved.

I constructed the policeman with a spike beneath his feet so he could be stuck in the lawn, and his right hand, held up for signaling a halt, was notched so it could hold the nozzle of a hose for watering lawns. He was my first project in wood-working class. I made other items, but the policeman has lasted.

He did his duty until Dad sold the house. All those 40 years of use he had been out there in the weather and had faded and chipped badly. Too, Nevada is a very dry state, and the pine from which he was made had dried and turned almost powdery.

When I got him to San Jose, he was sanded smooth, weather cracks filled, soaked in linseed oil to refresh the wood and later repainted.

He, as noted, is due for another full treatment and restoration this summer. A seventy year period of duty (though he is now merely decorative) ought to be rewarded.

I have a color photograph of him so that I can remember his countenance and other features.

The Map

When, in my youth, I was visiting my friend Don Lightfoot's house, I discovered a trove of information I have already mentioned, Mr. Lightfoot's National Geographic magazines. I was nine when I discovered a large world map folded in one of the magazines. Mr. Lightfoot had left all the maps in all the issues. I asked if I might have the large world map. He said I could. I took it home and mounted it in the kitchen behind the wood box near the old kitchen range.

That was the year that Ethiopia was invaded by the Italian army and the Emperor of Ethiopia, Haile Selassie, achieved public fame by appearing before the League of Nations to explain that if Mussolini was not stopped, WWII would surely follow. It did! Too, that was the period when Japan was about the business of invading China.

That very Christmas, I asked for and received a small Montgomery Ward table radio. It cost $9.95, a considerable sum in those days. It had tubes, a plastic case in imitation wood, and five push buttons. I was allowed to listen to the Richfield Reporter at 10:00 p.m. each evening. It was a fifteen-minute news broadcast which was the normal length of news broadcasts way back then. The program caught my attention because it was announced with a blare of trumpets.

In the matter of the map, I asked my dad if he could put some kind of cork backing behind my kitchen map of the world, which he did. I bought colored thumbtacks at the Sprouse-Reitz dime store, and started marking the progress of the Italian war in Ethiopia and the Japanese war in China based on the Richfield Reporter broadcasts. It was then the world was 'shocked' by the Japanese barbarically bombing cities. The shock did not last very long.

With the arrival of 1939 and the opening of WWII, my map began to be filled with a lot of colored tacks and I recall tracking the German conquests until, when I was 17, I graduated from Sparks High and joined the Navy V-5 aviation program. Later, I shifted to the V-12 program because it would provide a complete college degree and I knew that was one thing my family could not afford.

Whether we felt guilty or not about being in college during the war I'm not prepared to say.

But we did have a somewhat cynical slogan we batted around, 'Victory in 12 years or we fight!'

When I returned from WWII, the map was still on the wall and the colored tacks just where I had left them when I enlisted. Mother, however, had tacked a large letter 'V' over both Germany and Japan. The 'V,' she explained, was not for Victory, but for Vanquished.

I suspect I learned more geography from my map adventures than in school, though due to the various wars that were raging, some attention was paid to the matter in our history classes. Geography in those days was integrated into the high school history courses on the grounds it was wise to know where something occurred as well as when it occurred. The where, it was explained, could often give the answer to the why question.

Wallpapering

Dad did most of the painting and carpentry and plumbing inside and outside the house, though I gradually took over some of the duties when I got into my teens.

When Mother decided she wanted several of the rooms wallpapered because the old lath and plaster walls had developed unsightly cracks over the years and the repairs showed even when the walls had been repainted, Dad insisted it was a job he could readily do. Mother, who had read a book on how to do proper wallpapering, surrendered reluctantly.

Dad decided that the best and quickest method would be to paste up several long sheets of paper, then set them aside and put them up one at a time thereafter. Mother suggested that would make the waiting strips of paper too soggy, and they would be harder to handle. One strip at a time was what the wallpaper book recommended she said.

Dad chose to ignore the advice. He put a few sawhorses in the living room, placed two 8' by 4' sheets of plywood on top and pasted three or four rolls at a time.

The first strip went up well enough, but the second strip, sitting aside too long, had indeed gotten soggy and as Dad attempted to push the paper over his head with his fingers outward, instead of flat and parallel with his palms, his hands broke through and the wet paper slid down onto his head which, in its turn, perforated the paper such that wallpaper paste streamed down the back of his neck and under his collar.

Mother sat on the sofa and burst into laughter. I could not suppress myself either. Dad seethed!

When he had finally untangled himself and tossed the extra paper strips away he admitted, 'Well, Peggy, I suppose you had better do it yourself.'

Mother did all the wallpapering thereafter over a period of several years and an assignment of several rooms. She got quite good at the job.

The only time I worried was when she was papering the walls of the dormer above the stairs to our rooms. That required perilous positioning. She used a small three-foot ladder, put one high-heeled shoe on the flat banister around the landing, and the other on the dormer window ledge, and papered away. It was the one instance when I preferred not to watch — it seemed far too dangerous for my taste.

Our ceilings were 10 feet high so I got used to Mother standing on a ladder and leaning perilously this way or that.

I was commandeered to assist by virtue of setting up two sawhorses and only one plywood sheet, cutting strips (using a square) where she had marked, pasting them only when directed, and then handing them up to her on a ladder poised, as she often was, somewhere in outer space.

That was how I learned the details of the wallpapering art, including washing the excess paste off the paper, using a single-edged razor blade to let air out of any pockets that might have formed and pressing a sheet firmly against the wall with a special soft brush. Sometimes I had to make a small 'X' with the razor and insert a bit of extra past with my fingers.

It remains my life-long conviction that the only reason our ceilings did not earlier on cave in was they were held firmly in place by several layers of sturdy wallpaper.

Mr. Sam

When I was fourteen or fifteen years old, I cannot quite remember, my mother decided it was time for me to learn to travel, in this instance, to San Francisco for a week in the city, alone, by train. My father was against this, but Mother overruled him. Dad was rather afraid of cities. Mother, on the other hand, a world traveler in her younger days, was not.

Dad walked me to the station and the awaiting train (101, as I recall — a train made up of passenger and Pullman cars). I was put in the charge of Mr. Sam, a tall, black, porter with silver hair and enormous dignity. No one who worked on the railroad or anyone else for that matter called him just Sam. That would have been an affront to his dignity and his position. It was not that he ever demanded it, merely that his aura commanded it.

It fell upon Mr. Sam, to see that I was comfortably housed in my lower birth, at which time he explained to me that a 'gentleman' always had his shoes shined and, if necessary, his suit pressed so that he would be 'unwrinkled' on arrival at his destination. The shoe shining tip, I was advised, should be 50 cents for this particular train. If it happened to be the Streamliner, on the other hand, the tip should be $1. To over-tip, Mr. Sam explained was insulting. I had the wit not to ask why, since it was not necessary. I could tell by his air, and the sniff regarding the matter, that he was never to be considered to be in a menial position, but rather a deliverer of courteous service. There was a price, but it should not be overblown. Gentlemen did not do that.

At the dining car, I was placed under the jurisdiction of a waiter, a friend of Mr. Sam's named Walter, who went through, in some detail, the layout of the table and the silverware, what fork or other piece of equipment was to be used, and when and how to signal a waiter when some special attention was required. I absorbed the most of it.

By the time I arrived in Oakland and took the ferry across the Bay to San Francisco, I had been thoroughly educated in the matter of that form and manner of travel which separates the gentleman from the ordinary boor. I cannot (half a century later) remember Mr. Sam's exact words, but the gist of it was that if you acted the gentleman, you would be treated as the gentleman, and if you had a natural, quiet expectation of service, you would receive it promptly and with the appropriate solicitude.

After crossing the Bay, I took an 'N' streetcar to the Shaw Hotel just off Market Street (somewhere around Geary, as I recall). I was expected (Dad was very thorough) at the 'railroad man's' hotel.' By the way, the mattresses (I think straw) were harder than the pavement on Market Street. I did enjoy lying in bed during the night, though, listening to the streetcars clanging their bells as they went by, and to the electric hum and overhead sparking which accompanied their progress.

In the morning, to my surprise, San Francisco's streets and sidewalks were wet with night moisture (we did not have much of that in Nevada). I was genuinely thrilled to find a chain of coffee shops with deep orange upholstery and wonderful hot cakes. I think the name was Maxwell's or some such thing. I know that's not quite it, but I'm having another senior memory moment.

Down the street a mere hop and skip was the Golden Gate theatre at which a movie was playing and Miss Sally Rand was dancing after. I was a little startled that I was let in with no questions asked. But, given that Miss Rand, when she finally parted her fans, was on a stairway at the very back of the stage some enormous distance from the audience, under a dim blue spotlight and was probably wearing a body stocking, I can't say there was anything prurient about the matter. The lady did dance gracefully.

San Francisco had its little peculiarities. I was startled to find that a restaurant named the 'City of Paris,' was Italian, complete with checkered tablecloths (red wine at the table without any question). I indulged in a glass — my very first. There were singing waiters with white napkins over their arms hovering uncomfortably close and being overly attentive. It seemed to me to be very elegant, but the truth was, I felt more comfortable in the coffee shops. A bit of neglect can sometimes be a good thing.

I did have a happy time going hither and thither on either the Key System (a light rail that seemed to go everywhere) to visit my Aunt Annie in Oakland, and on the streetcars to the Franklin Hospital where my sister was in nurse training.

There was a park named Sutro's along the seacoast. And on that trip I remember taking my first roller-coaster ride made really frightening by the fact that the area wasn't all that well lit and the ups, downs, and curves were a total surprise.

Mr. Sam was not on 102 going the other way when I finally caught the train for home. But, now reasonably well trained in the matters of tips and decorum, I seemed to manage well enough. I made other trips and met Mr. Sam once more on one of them. He had neither aged nor lost any of his inherent dignity. His greeting, of course, was warm but subdued, as mine was expected to be.

Thinking it over, some people are born to the aristocracy. Other good people are natural aristocrats. Mr. Sam was of the latter group.

Duties

It was one of my duties to carry the garbage out to the back fence along the alley and put it in one of the garbage pails (tin, not plastic) that were kept out there. This was an evening chore to be completed on a daily basis immediately after the dinner cleanup had ended.

We did not have a dish washer, so my older sister washed the dishes and my younger sister wiped them. After we had all left home, of course, the chores reverted to the original owners. It seemed to be a time for conversation on their part and the reviewing of the day, so my parents never bothered to get one of those modern devices.

Early on we did not have a furnace, but rather a wood/coal stove in the living room and a wood/coal range in the kitchen. My job was to empty the ashes first thing in the morning and, when Dad was away from home, build the fires in both stoves (all year in the kitchen and seasonally in the living room). Too, I chopped the mill blocks, filled the wood box and loaded the coal scuttle.

Our property was about seventy-five feet wide and about one-hundred-fifty feet deep. We had two lawns in the back, another large one along the biggest side of the house, a narrower one along the other side, and two smaller lawns in front. Too, there was the long parkway. We had two hand mowers, one sixteen and the other twenty inches wide. I, earlier on, preferred the lighter, smaller mower with the metal wheels. The wide one with the big rubber tires came into use later as I entered my teens. The mowing chore was a weekly one which I did on Friday evenings or very early Saturday morning so as not to interfere with my own lawn-mowing business which took up most of Saturday and most of Sunday.

I mowed our lawns as a duty. For others I charged a fee. My basic charge was 25 cents, but for cross-mowing (giving that golf-green smoothness), I charged 50 cents. Most of my customers liked the fancier work, since I clipped extra carefully for that enormous sum and even did a spot of weeding as required.

Sometimes, people would move into a house that had not been rented for a while and I would earn as much as $10 or $15 for clearing out a front or back yard (or both) that had gone to tumble weeds and other varieties. This was often a week-long task, using my early and late weekday hours and any spare time I could gather up on weekends.

I gave up all that labor gradually when I got hired as to mop the floors and act as stock boy at the local Sprouse-Reitz five-and-dime store. For a while I tried to manage to keep the mowing too, but began to gather more and more hours at the store as I took over some of the shelf arranging, reordering and, when things were pressing, one of the cash registers.

I worked at Sprouse-Reitz before school (opening the store and stocking the cash registers) at 7:00-8:15 and after (from 4:30-7:00, or until I finished stocking shelves and ordering). On Saturdays I worked a full twelve hours (or longer during the holiday seasons). The going minimum wage in those days was 37 ½ cents an hour. I found myself reasonably wealthy.

I also was sent to the local grocery store from time to time for something that had not gotten included in my mother's telephone ordering and the store's Saturday deliveries. And, earlier on, when the Depression was deepest, I would pedal my bike to the Zenclusen farm and get eggs at 10 cents the dozen and Mrs. Zenclusen's home-made bread at 5 cents a loaf. Milk was delivered by the milkman, in glass bottles, and was 6 cents a quart.

When we finally got a washing machine, it fell upon my sisters to take the clothes, in a wicker basket, and hang them on the line for drying. We had, as I remember, three long clothes lines that stretched from the back of the house to a wooden bar nailed to the original big wood shed and later to the garage. Sometimes I had to trail my sisters with the clothespin bag as they retrieved the dried sheets and other laundry. Everything, of course, smelled very fresh.

The clothes were still hung out on the lines during the winter, because Nevada is very dry and the clothes would, very modernly, 'freeze dry,' and were perfect, as they thawed indoors, for ironing, or so my mother used say.

Mother, after we got an electric iron to replace the old sad irons, was something of a hazard, as she would sometimes absentmindedly lay the hot iron across its own cord. From time to time, this caused great blue sparks, and I had to progress to the hardware store to buy a new cord and replacement fuses. In those days, the separate cord plugged into the iron as is no longer the case with our modern appliances.

When we got the electric stove, Mother was still something of a hazard. Since the stove gave off little heat other than to the burners, she sometimes would lay a dish towel on a burner that had not been turned off or that had not yet cooled down. Her luck held, and the place never went up in flames to match my father's frequent predictions

Super Dad

My dad was a small man, just 5' 4" but very strong, sometimes amazingly so.

When it came time to replace the big, black, pot-bellied living room stove with an elegant, 'modern,' imitation-wood model (with an isinglass window so we could see the flames inside) Dad cleared a path from the living room to the garage by propping doors open and then, ignoring my mother's cautions, he picked up the stove around its middle and in one long march hauled it out of the house, down the steps, and put it is the garage where he had made a space for it. There it remained until the house was sold.

Earlier, he had given a similar performance in removing the old kitchen stove, another black monster, and replacing it with an ivory and tan 'modern' wood and coal range. I was present for the assembly of that wonderful object and cautioned not to hang onto the chromium bar that passed across the oven of the stove to take care of such matters as drying towels and other such items.

Dad had eight brothers of various ages. All of them were ordered to settle their differences by my fierce and tiny grandmother with boxing gloves provided for that occasion. So, Dad admitted, they all became rather handy with their fists.

This was a good thing, because there was one colleague of Dad's on the railroad known for his terrible outbursts of temper and assaults on his fellow workers. His name was Rex D.

One time Dad came home with some serious bruises on his face. In answer to Mother's queries he noted that Rex D. had made the mistake of losing his temper with him.

'What happened,' Mother asked.

'He challenged me,' Dad noted. 'I detest bullies.'

'So?' Mother queried.

'So he lost and he won't be bullying anybody for a while,' Dad growled. Nothing more was said.

At the far end of our double living room rested a heavy, square, grand piano which had come along with the house. When it was necessary to insert a carpet underneath the front legs of the piano, Dad would get on his knees, crawl toward the center of the piano and then raising his back lift the entire front. Mother could then slide the carpet under the raised legs.

I remember that the piano was sufficiently heavy as to cause the pine flooring immediately below it to sag somewhat. I was present when Dad crawled under the house to erect 4" by 4" post braces under the flooring.

Dad also conducted an eternal war against dandelions. It was common to see him out there on the lawns, in a squatting position, for several hours, digging up the offending weeds.

Even in my teens I found it sometimes difficult to rise to a standing position after a long weeding session of that sort. It seemed to leave Dad unaffected, even into his seventies when he would, on a visit here, perform similar activities on our lawns. I suppose I should credit all that gardening, railroading, building, and lifting, as contributing to his excellent physical condition. And, of course, he walked everywhere without thought or complaint.

Games

Modern times have interfered with, or made redundant many types of games. I suppose they have been replaced by all those electronic devices which require keen eyes, quick finger dexterity, and sitting, sitting, sitting.

Our games, in an earlier day, were considerably more athletic — 'Run Sheep Run,' 'Kick the

Can' and 'Hide and Seek.' Of course, we had the advantage of dirt streets, a single bulb with a white metal reflector on top of a corner telephone pole as our sole evening and night light. This made such games relatively easy to play — that is, we were able to hide fairly close to home base, rush in and kick the can before it could be kicked away, or avoid being tagged when headed for home base, or get home 'free' in the case of 'Run Sheep Run.'

We also required dirt for Mumble Peg and for marbles, though a lawn was quite acceptable for Mumble Peg, a game involving the use of a pocket knife (at least the one we played) and the ability to toss it up in the air with this or that spin and have it land upright and sticking into the soil.

For marbles, we had but to draw a circle in the dirt. Our marbles were mostly 'aggies' (glass type). But the occasional opponent had a large steely (ball bearing) and could vengefully fracture are more fragile aggies.

Our construction hobbies were somewhat more complex than the current models, at least in terms of getting things cut out and glued together. We could buy kits which were made up of thin sheets of balsa wood on which the various airplane parts were outlined. It was left to us to use single edged razor blades (few could afford any of these modern hobby cutting knives) to carve out the parts without breaking them. Assembly was more complex and involved gluing and holding with airplane glue

— a clear fast drying element that it never once occurred to us to inhale. Then, there was the matter of cutting and gluing the thin tissue paper on the frame of the airplane. This was followed by 'doping' — putting a thin kind of shellac on the tissue paper which tightened it nicely and gave it a sturdier surface and a welcome sheen.

Some of the simpler aircraft involved a single sturdy shaft with a pair of long, thin, rubber bands stretched lightly from the propeller hook to the special hook attached just underneath the tail. The propeller was spun around (with one's index finger) until the rubber bands were as tightly wound as possible (without snapping the spine of the airplane). Then the craft was pointed upward and let go. Depending on the size of the plane and the length of it (for better rubber bands), we could get heady altitudes. Naturally, our airplanes frequently crashed, and this meant returning to the drawing board for repairs and maintenance.

Our plane flying and kite flying required a good deal of running and other outdoor exercise, as likewise did the various tag games we played under the street light of an early winter evening. We were more inclined to play the night games in fall and winter, as it got dark earlier, and we were not required to get to bed before the light had gone.

In the summer we made do with baseball and a rather strange kind of soccer game in which we drove dried tumbleweeds toward a goal. For this game we used broom handles and a great deal of enthusiasm. A lot of 'cracked' ankles and sore shins resulted.

Those same broom handles could also be equipped with a hand guard (simple crosspiece nailed near the top of the handle). When we wound friction tape above the guard we felt we had created a reasonable facsimile of a sword. We did a lot of dueling whenever one of the pirate movies came out starring Errol Flynn or Tyrone Power.

We also were able, most times, during the late summer, to find a willow patch and make proper whips that we could crack. Clyde Beatty, the lion tamer was our model. Lions and tigers being somewhat scarce in Sparks, we were inclined to frequently substitute ourselves in the animal roles.

As a result of all this, we were mostly a thin looking lot with ravenous appetites as a result and did not (except for such horrors as liver) need a lot of encouragement in the matter of eating heartily.

Earlier on, those of us who lived east of 15th street had to haul our scooters two blocks to the high school and junior high because the block those two buildings were on had genuine sidewalks. Too, when the tennis nets were down (or not), we used the paved courts between the two buildings for our scooting.

Ultimately, we were grateful for the WPA and Mr. Roosevelt, because sidewalks were installed all the way to 20th street to the east and Prater Way to the north. Shortly after, the streets were paved and we had to find empty dirt lots for our marble games.

Expectations

One of the expectations most of us now older folk had in our youth was a prayer for a Dickens Christmas in terms of snowy weather. There was something very chancy about the weather in those days. It was not predicted. No one had the tools to make prognostications other than those elderly folk with rheumatism who were alleged to be able to tell when it was going to rain — rare in Nevada — or get cold — not uncommon. Otherwise, weather, if any, simply rolled in over the Sierras and we dealt with it on arrival.

Mostly the skies of my youth were brilliantly blue and cloudless. I could ride my bicycle to the Zenclusen ranch, borrow one of the older horses, and make a journey into sagebrush country without any concern for rain or other interferences, though there could be a fall of as much as sixty degrees between mid-afternoon and night temperatures and one had better be prepared. Too, the desert being dry and water holes scarce, one took along one of those canvas bags of water (for the loyal steed) and a large metal canteen in one of the saddle bags.

As I've noted, one of our common childhood hopes was for snow at Christmas, most particularly Christmas Eve. We were lucky in the matter about one time out of five when genuine weather rolled in and we were treated to frosted window panes and the scene of accumulating snow, gently heaping itself on top of the pickets on the front fence (our critical measure of depth).

When it did snow and the sun warmed things a little, followed by a freeze, we earned a treat — icicles appeared on the eaves of the house. Some of them were marvelously long. We used them for sword fights. They were fragile, and such crossing of swords as we could manage never resulted in any serious harm. Of course, we also treated the occasional icicle as a Popsicle despite maternal warnings that the water came from the roof and the icicles doubtless were steeped with dirt, and other dangerous elements, and we would come down with some dreaded bug. We never did. Dad kept the cedar shingles (the old-fashioned flat kind) regularly oiled and germs did not seem to want to live there.

Icicles, on occasion, made excellent snowmen noses and, pushed in deeply, ears. Deeper yet, glistening buttons down the tummy. But we preferred coal for the buttons and a carrot (dug out of the frozen ground) for a nose. Corn husks made marvelous elfin ears. Dad was not always pleased, however, to find we had used his spare 'work' hat for our snowman. The weather eventually warmed up, the old fellow, no matter how large, waned and fell over in a fractured heap. Very sad, though the corpse could provided snow for snowballs and was sometimes integrated into a fort.

Though I'm sure nostalgia tempers all reality, I sometimes miss the seasons.

There were, in and around Sparks, a few natural ponds which happily froze hard in the winter. We had ice skates, not the shoe type (much too expensive for infrequent use), but the type that clamped on to the soles of shoes or, better yet, boots. The boots, tightly laced, helped in removing the curse of ankle wobble and strain which eventually ended long-term skating for those who had to rely on shoes. I think we were departing childhood by the time my sisters and I received our first shoe skates and naturally and alas, we were immediately treated to two or three 'abnormally warm' winters wherein such ice as we could find was thin and ill made.

When I was younger, I was also taken on the occasional journey to Lake Tahoe by the families of friends who had automobiles and enjoyed the properly named Emerald Bay. Mr. Lightfoot was the local Scout Master and father of my pal Don, so I enjoyed extra outdoor adventures and camping trips.

Summer looming, swimming was mostly in large ponds formed by the currents of the Truckee

River. It was not until I was in high school that Sparks sprang for a swimming pool. Since it was but two blocks north of our house, I haunted the place during the summer months, right up to the time when I left to join the Navy.

Youth, and I believe it was better then than now, had the constant blessing of hope, but not the chain of professional prediction. Hope brings joy. But prediction, often, brings disappointment.

Ghosts of Past Christmases

The ghosts of past Christmases do not come my way during the middle of the night, and never with the idea of reformation, since it is far too late for that. In my case at least, the ghosts have to be deliberately conjured, and there is only one fleeting instant when they can be rounded up.

When the Christmas tree has been put in place, the lights attached, and the ornaments hung, then the proper moment is not far away. I wait until everyone else has gone to bed, then walk into the darkened living room and turn on only the Christmas lights. Thus, I can stand back in the room and concentrate on the glitter in the midst of the deep shadows that omit the walls and most of the furniture, and construct a return glimpse of yesterday's other trees and other times — most often my childhood days when there was a purity of anticipation unsullied by much of a knowledge of the world or all the wrongs within. As far as

I knew, a fellow named Claus handled all the economic matters.

It's a fleeting experience at best and there is no way I can now, after all these years, distinguish one Christmas scene from another in terms of actual years. On one occasion I received an electric train. On an earlier date (but I know not how much) I received a Mickey Mouse movie camera with several brief and silent films of Mickey Mouse and Charlie Chase and the Three Stooges. I was delighted, and played the movies over and over again most of that day and several of those that followed. These are images that pop up unbidden of other years.

I can't conjure up a specific Christmas or a specific toy or set of toys. It is by chance that the Christmas when I received a much-wanted erector set once popped up, and too, the patient building of an eight-floor elevator with a motor which I used to haul my younger sister's miniature dolls up and down at her request. I have a brief glimmer of building a giant Ferris wheel on which the dolls could ride. Then the scene was gone and there was little use in trying to evoke another. Perhaps next year when the tree is ready it will happen again or perhaps not.

And what happened this very evening when the winds were whipping about the house and threatening the neighborhood trees? This memory went back to my Tom Thumb typewriter, a dial-a-

letter affair with a soft, purple-inked roller.
There was a large lever to push below the dial.
Pick a letter, push the lever, and print a character
on a small piece of paper. Certainly, it was not a
fast process, but I remember being delighted with
it. It is inherent in these flashes that something
not thought of and which could not have been
deliberately conjured (the purple-inked roller)
always arrives.

The images are not mere memories, however, but
rather vivid momentary pictures in full color, and I
can tell you the details of the tree or the room and
the metal petals around the Christmas light shields
(which got hot), the angel (on that occasion) with
the spun-glass gown. Sometimes they seem to be a
montage, sometimes not. Their one grand quality
is that for a few moments (or, more realistically
seconds) I'm devoid of all the accumulations of
adulthood and all the encrustations of the years.

For a moment or two the joy is a pure and
unsullied as it was then and that's enough. What
will the next year bring? Not to worry or to
wait. All of my ghosts, like Dickens's third, are
inherently mercurial.

Hello and Goodbye

It is one thing to recall a favorite publication
which has faded away from one's daily life such as
the 'Saturday Evening Post.' It was first published,
after all, in 1821 and ran steadily on until 1969.

Then it was resurrected, to appear less frequently from 1971 to the present.

But to hear, some years ago, that 'Life' magazine was shutting down (to reappear on special occasion a la the 'Post') was more of a blow, since I can recall the first appearance on or near my 11th birthday (November 1936), which means I was at least competent to pour through its photographs and pages, and did so whenever I could find a copy.

It was that same year (1936) that my mother began to subscribe to the 'Saturday Evening Post' and 'Better Homes & Gardens,' which meant we were unusually prosperous. Prior to that, I read magazines at wealthier friend's houses, and this remained true for 'Life' and 'National Geographic.'

My mother was saddened to bid goodbye to 'the Post.' She held on to her subscription to 'Better Homes & Gardens' until she died, and Dad carried on until he died.

Even in the 1930's, radio was becoming the general source of information and the magazines were beginning to specialize. Our first radio arrived in 1933. I'm certain it was March that year, because the first thing we listened to was Franklin Roosevelt's Inaugural Address. The voice was unforgettable.

Our radio was a table model with a curved top. I believe it was a 'Majestic.' Dad had to put an antenna (a long wire) along the eaves on three sides of the house in order to pull in Reno seven miles away.

Speed Henry

Way back there in the twenties and thirties, we had three ready examples of what we thought to be high technology: automobiles, airplanes and giant steam locomotives, the latter slightly smaller versions of the monster locomotive on the Union Pacific known as 'Big Boy.'

I was pushing on toward two years of age when Charles Lindbergh made his famous solo flight across the Atlantic. But his fame and his adventure hung on a good while, and he became a part of that set of my childhood heroes who included Admiral Byrd, Tom Mix, and 'Speed' Henry, the SP engineer who lived across the street from us.

Speed Henry was the head 'hog head.' That is, he drove the leading giant engine with another one right behind, one in the center of the train and one bringing up the rear. The four engineers had to be, and were, highly skilled at coordination. Even then, one or more of the driving wheels of the engines might slip a bit on the initial movement of the train and make a stream of sparks.

It was my custom to walk from our house to the western end of the switching yard (some three blocks south and watch the final preparations for the assault on the Sierras. It was particular fun in the winter because the train was often preceded by a giant snow-blowing locomotive clearing a path. The snow was hurled into the air about half a block from the railroad tracks. It made, when there were heavy snows, wonderful hills near the tracks for sledding. We were forbidden to get any nearer than that, and most of us had enough sense to obey the order.

Speed Henry was well aware of his celebrity status. It was his habit to have his starched coveralls, cap and gloves delivered to the yard office where he changed from a business suit to the proper uniform. He would prowl about his engine, with oil can in hand as a group of us gathered in admiration. Then he would board his train, send out a great side blast of steam, make a few hand signals to the engines behind, and wave to us as the four great engines began the coordinated movement of the train.

Mr. Henry, a modern sort of fellow, had a Vespa scooter he used to get to and fro from work. He owned an automobile, but did not use it very often. He also had a small dog of Heinz origins who rode behind him on the scooter. The dog always found his way home on his own. The dog, like his master, also drank beer. Speed would pour a little of his beer in a small dish and the dog would lap it up joyfully.

I did not meet Tom Mix, Mr. Lindbergh or Admiral Byrd, but I read books about them, and they seemed as well delineated and heroic as Speed Henry. I was long beyond childhood (and am grateful) before my heroes began to show clay feet. Tom Mix was put down frequently. Mr. Lindbergh was much maligned because of his alleged affection for the Nazis and his 'America first' associations. Later books questioned the intents, value and purposes of even Admiral Byrd. Speed Henry, only locally famous, remained as we imagined him, his exploits remembered, his character sound. Well, there was, of course, my mother's disapproval of allowing a dog to take to drink.

Home Construction

I have mentioned our joy at moving into the final home of our childhood. But that certainly did not end it.

Dad's first major alteration of the premises was to replace, with wall plugs, the electric cords that hung from the center of the 12-foot ceilings of all the rooms, at the end of which was a glass shade and a light bulb. He converted the hanging light in the kitchen to a proper ceiling fixture, and though we had few appliances, sprinkled a lot of wall sockets around in case we ever did. Oddly, Mr. Englekey, being electrically impaired, had not wired the upstairs rooms but had left them to the warm glow of kerosene lamps.

Dad considered this 'asking for it,' and wired our rooms too.

His second major construction was to add a sun porch extension to the kitchen's South end. He had acquired a host of wooden passenger-car windows from the railroad wrecking yards and, mounted them in vertical pairs, creating a light and sun-lit room. Between each of the sets of two vertical windows we eventually installed brackets and glass shelves so my mother could fill the spaces with small, potted, blooming houseplants. In the process, he turned the stairs from one pantry entry so they opened onto the new sun porch.

There was a ceiling register above the living room stove so my sister's room was heated. Mine remained comfortable only to the extent warmth rose up the stairwell and into my room, which may explain, in the winter mornings, why I would rise from bed, grab my clothes, sprint down the stairs to the warmth of the kitchen, and dress while parked on the wood box.

Dad was a great builder of fires. By the time I rose in the morning, the left side of the kitchen stove was a glowing dim red, to say nothing of the first foot or two of the stovepipe which came out of the back of the stove, turned, and then marched upward toward the ceiling, turned again, and entered the central chimney above the water heater by the wood box.

Of a really cold winter morning, when even the top of the wood box might have been called chilly, I would pick up my clothes, run down the stairs to the kitchen, and stand just by the glowing stove pipe where it exited the stove. That was most likely the warmest place in town. But there was a catch. Sometimes, when donning my pants, I bent over a bit carelessly and singed my tail on the glowing stove pipe which, because it was turning upward, was ribbed. This left scars, some of which remain to this day and bring an occasional inquiry during one of my physical exams. 'Stove pipes,' I Always respond. But today's doctors are younger and, not wishing to appear ignorant, rarely pursue the matter.

The kitchen-bathroom door was always left open at those times to gather up such heat (and there was plenty) as it could. The water heater, not insulated, also added warmth to the kitchen.

But there were always cold areas in the house during the winter — those corners and crevices a good distance from either stove. Still, there's something special about the heat of a wood/coal fire that brings you to its vicinity and allows you, in terms of distance, to select the comfort zone you prefer.

Another of Dad's great projects was the replacement, with concrete walks, of the wooden planks that led from the front porch to the street (we had no sidewalks or curbs as the streets were not yet paved) and from the back porch to the tool shed and wood shed. He built the forms and mixed the cement in a wheelbarrow, did the pouring, and we leveled everything by see-sawing a two-by-four the length of each walk after it had been poured. Then, Dad finished the work with a trowel and an edger he had rounded up one way or another

Eventually, the City of Sparks decided to pave its residential streets and put in curbs and sidewalks. The assessment per household was horrendous - - $100 for a fifty-foot-wide lot and $125 for a seventy-five-foot one. We got hit for $125. Dad griped, but, like all the others, we paid. The twenty-five foot lot which Dad had bought (for $75 the previous year) was lower than the rest of the property, so Dad, with a fifth of good bourbon and a glib tongue, persuaded the man who ran the grader to push the excess soil into the sunken lot until it was properly even.

A couple of other people with sunken lots on the same street bitched to the City fathers about my dad's privileged arrangement. Wise in their own way and realizing they would save a good deal of money in not having to haul off the scrapings, the city fathers surrendered. The operator of the grader was, Dad said, thoroughly groused because the others did not provide bottles of good bourbon. 'That's the way of it,' Dad explained. 'Some people always want something for nothing.'

Eventually, Dad got around to modernizing the bathroom. The great claw-footed bath tub, the claws resting on large round crystals, was removed and replaced with a modern, shorter, square tub. The ceiling-high walnut box that contained the water that flushed the toilet by means of a chain and a fancy knob at the end was removed and 'modern' facilities replaced it. The bathroom was tiled with a 'new' type of plastic tile. A fancy wash basin was also installed. People would later pay dearly for examples of the antiques Dad ripped out and discarded. And so it went, through the forty years.

I don't really believe we ever know or truly understand our parents. I thought Dad enjoyed all those years of continual construction. He admitted before he died, that he hated it. I laughed and told him he had thoroughly deceived me and, for good or ill, taught me to enjoy painting, plumbing (though plumbing not lately), wallpapering and repairs, and that I was grateful because it saved me a small fortune and filled me with many contented moments.

'Well,' I said, 'at least you had the garden and enjoyed that, what with being featured in Better Homes & Gardens a couple of years running.'

'I didn't like gardening either,' he admitted. 'But your mother loved flowers. I did it for her.'

Some parental gifts are inadvertent. I enjoy gardening.

Isolation

A city such as Sparks, not very large and not very wide, could be deserted almost as quickly as you please with a fifteen minute bicycle ride, or preferably, a horse. You could see the high Sierras easily to the west and great open desert expanses to the north, east, and south. What is more, you could get there from wherever your own personal here happened to be and quickly find yourself in a special kind of isolation — not a living human soul about.

This meant that should you encounter almost anyone (a rare event) in the desert or the countryside, you made some kind of pleasant exchange. Mostly I ran into a rancher or a farmer scouting his territory for broken fences or wandered cattle. The greeting was usually 'howdy' followed by an inquiry of how things were going in 'town.' In my case that meant Sparks. If there happened to be any special news such as the local theatre or the city hall burning down (which happened) I conveyed the news. Otherwise, 'fine' was sufficient.

I believe the great empty spaces and the kind of aloneness and isolation that brings marks one, if he is reared under such circumstances, to a different type of mind to those who are city bred and who also are isolated while being embedded.

To achieve isolation in a crowded area like a city, one must develop a special kind of indifference to the masses around him. The passers by, and even the immediate neighbors, are not usually known, deliberately so — human ships passing each other on the special seas of conscious indifference.

In the rural areas nature was not feared, but respected. In our more rural days it was the city which was the sight of hazard and of sin. These days, with variations, the countryside is the home of camps and frightening nature where werewolves and villains with knives (Jason) normally appear and slaughter those who prefer to go off alone and naked for a swim in the night. It is the modern equivalent of the silly woman in a negligee who used to go, in the old movies, candle in hand, into some windy secret passage behind the mansion's bookcases.

In the wide open spaces of my youth, being alone meant you had better know something about the areas you had chosen to wander in. Help was never immediate. Cell phones were unknown. A patrolling policemen or ambulances did not venture that way. Bitten by a rattlesnake or a scorpion, you'd better have come equipped to slit the wound, evacuate the poison, and return to home base. A small home-assembled first-aid kit was to go armed against misadventure.

To ride into the desert country without a canteen would have been considered sheer madness. And, armed with a rifle, one might slay an animal that threatened without even a distant dream of anything called animal rights or rampant animal rightists. That would have been considered comic.

The city life, I'd venture, is quite another matter. Masses of men and women daily come and go on their own errands, usually indifferent to those around them unless they are of some macabre appearance or action and even then, the movement is not toward but away. Some areas in the city are dangerous not because of an indifferent nature but rather because of deliberate malice. It requires a wariness of a different kind.

All this leads up, I'd say, to the fact that those folk from the rural areas do indeed have a different cast of mind than those in the city. What is the title for the latter habitat, 'the lonely crowd?' I'd go farther and say the larger the city the more actual the indifference and the more artificial the public caring. Or just maybe, lacking actual intimacy, the pretense of loss, such as flowers along the roadside for an unknown victim, is necessary. It is not so much a matter of humanity as it is of desperate need.

Kantian Times

I'm not certain whether or not my mother read Kant, but I rather think she did. Dad had not for certain, but he was Kantian nonetheless, at least in his firm believe in duty rather than happiness.

I cannot recall my mother or my father ever evincing the slightest interest in my psychic development beyond the fact that they had very firm notions about the family's 'good name' and any behavior that might otherwise put a blot on it. About this they seemed adamant, and when that principle was violated, justice was swift, terrible and physical. Mother used a wire-handled flyswatter (the wire end). Dad threatened to and sometimes did 'cuff behind the ears.' Since he worked outdoors for the Southern Pacific Railroad and was a continuing gardener, his cuffs had a resounding quality about them. They set my head to ringing.

There was, in our household, a never mentioned, but omnipotent relationship between the cause and the effect. Early on, when I grew lazy or forgetful and did not have the wood box and coal scuttle filled before adjourning to bed, my father, next morning, would roust me to a cold house and mercilessly send me out to an even colder wood shed to chop the mill blocks and load the coal scuttle and haul them in before he built any fires. His discipline was sufficiently consistent that later, when I had forgotten my duty and could hear him slapping his hands together and rubbing them to ward off any possible chill (quite audible everywhere), I scooted out of bed and quickly dressed and hied myself off to the wood shed to do those duties earlier forgotten. An irritated cuff in the morning was not acceptable.

When Dad was on the Extra Board (on call at any indeterminate time), he would often sleep during the daytime since most of his calls were for night runs. We had a duty to remain quiet around the area of his bedroom window.

We learned rough and ready play in relative silence, as we did not want our play to turn out to be any rougher or readier. By the way, no such rule appeared when we were in bed. The back door could slam at any hour of the night or early morning and announce Dad was 'in from the road.' But, if it was at any reasonable morning hour, it meant he would make breakfast and that would mean hot cakes and Canadian bacon and syrup and other goodies.

His only flaw, to my memory, is that he always had the frying pan too hot when he made the eggs and they were always brown around the edges. Other than that, we had no complaints. Mother, you see, was inclined to serve Wheaties (which I happened to like) or Raisin Bran (which I detested). Raisins belonged in raisin toast and properly nowhere else.

Dad was always pushing oatmeal because it 'would stick to your ribs,' but I usually countered (having filled my plate with bacon, hot cakes and eggs), that I really did not want sticky ribs. He usually let this pass.

My mother had a number of sayings, one of which was that 'little pitchers have big ears.'

Accordingly, Dad was forbidden to swear around the house. On wounded or frustrating occasions (a misplaced hammer blow catching his thumb, for example) he confined himself to the expression, 'Sam Hill.'

Now, I admit, I do not know who Sam Hill was, though I have a vague idea that he had something to do with railroads or that, whoever he was, railroad men did not like him. I could be wrong.

Dad could utter those two words with sufficient steam behind them to singe the lawn for forty feet. Later, when I traveled with him 'on the road,' I discovered he had a much broader vocabulary in the matter of expletives which Mother had insisted always be deleted. They turned out useful, later, in the Navy. At least I was not shocked, save for the redundancy of it all.

Dad 'Sam Hilled' a lot when I was young, particularly on the occasion of my digging the elephant trap into which he fell one night, or the several times I erected various secret strings and methods of opening and closing the wood shed and the tool shed doors which, I might note, pulled in the wrong order caused great beams to fall into place and thoroughly lock them. Dad was mostly tolerant of this necessary string-pulling business except for the time when the water coils in the kitchen stove burst and sprayed the ceiling with ashes and he wanted his tools 'Johnny Quick' (another favorite of his terms). No, I don't know who Johnny Quick was either.

In the instance of the exploding water coils, defeated in his attempts to get into his own tool shed, he hurled me physically through the open window in front of the shed with instructions to open the door as quickly as possible. I moved very rapidly as I recall.

Chores were never open to discussion. We had duties and that was it. Mine included keeping the wood box and coal scuttles filled, weeding and watering the vegetable garden (no small spread) and mowing the lawns with a hand-mower on Saturdays. We had a very large lawn, at least four times the size of my current one.

We had two lawn mowers. My favorite had brass wheels (and treads) and cut a 16" swath. It was lighter than the other, which was 22" and had rubber tires. I also found that if I mowed the lawn on Saturday (with the grass catcher, which added to the load) and then again on Tuesday without the catcher, the job was quicker and easier over all.

The grass clippings were spread around the flower beds and between rows in the vegetable garden to dry out and, in the fall, be spaded into the soil. Waste not; want not. Since, when I grew older, one of my jobs in the fall was to spade all that grass under the soil, I managed to stay in reasonable physical shape.

Dad could repair almost anything, but always managed to have a few remaining 'unnecessary' parts left over. Accordingly, Mother usually asked me to fix the toaster or the vacuum cleaner or other devices while he was away. 'You,' she said, 'seem to manage without any remainders.' Indeed, I did. I had a fairly good memory and a decent geometric talent. Too, I usually laid parts out on a newspaper in the order I took them out of the machine under repair (first out, furthest away, last out nearest). This made reassembly easier.

As an ex-machinist, Dad was eternally saving money by making a faulty part on his own from the materials at hand. This did not always work well (created rather odd noises where none should be and hastened the demise of the device in question).

When I was repairing, Mother managed to come up with the money for a trip to Wards or Sears for the new part. This was a secret which was never announced to my father. As far as he knew, as I grew in years, the household appliances had a better record of survival. In that fashion, I learned most of the skills I now use to keep down the cost of repairs.

Early on, I found it interesting to watch other repairmen in the neighborhood going about their labors. Sometimes I offered to help and learned more than I gave. Those were the days when people could not afford to hire professionals and made do as best they could. I also, by the way, increased my profane vocabulary in no less than three languages.

Schools, teachers and homework more or less ruled our early years. I had no teacher who encountered any trouble from my parents. Teachers were in charge at school, and that was clearly that. One did not mention a disciplinary difficulty at school unless one wanted to have the whole thing repeated at home. That seemed like over-re-enforcement, so silence prevailed.

I admit to the dreaming of being the son of Nick and Nora Charles of 'The Thin Man' series. Imagine Dad being relaxed enough to shoot a dart pistol at his own tree ornaments. Imagine Dad spending his days lounging around the house in a smoking jacket, sipping martinis and being mellow. Imagine having a wealthy mother. Imagine having a detective couple for parents. Imagine clever Asta as a pet. Imagine what a pleasant life that would be.

But, in those days self-pity was frowned upon and one had to make do with the parents he had, and remember the sorry plight of 'The Little Match Girl,' who had none, and count one's blessings. I was not likely to freeze to death with the parents I had at hand.

Mechanical and Other Sentiments

Certain gadgets of the past can generate memories of either fondness or inconvenience. I actually think, in their simpler way, they were more convenient and less frustrating than some of their modern replacements.

The Brownie camera comes to mind. Mine was a somewhat rounded Bakelite box with a universal lens. I could not go too far away from or too near my subject. Otherwise, the pictures nearly always came out just right. The Brownie box camera cost $1.

The possession of the camera launched me into my own film-developing career complete with developing fluid, fixers, appropriate shallow plastic trays, shiny chromium sheets for producing glossies, a red light and a self-constructed darkroom made entirely of tar paper over slats, inside our wood shed and very hot indeed.

Since I was, much earlier, about the business of writing and distributing my productions, I had a form of copier (long since vanished) which consisted of either a special typewriter ribbon (I had an ancient portable), or special pencils. I typed or wrote out a sheet of paper and then, laid it on a shallow tray filled with a special kind of gelatin which absorbed the ink. I could then lay a sheet of paper on top of the gelatin, roll it lightly, wait a moment and peeling it off, have a reproduction.

Eventually, the ink sank to the bottom of the gelatin and I could produce a different master and repeat the process.

We finally got an electric toaster which replaced a wire rack we used on top of the wood stove. The new toaster was of a pyramid construction. You opened the sloping doors on each side, placed the bread slices on them and closed them. You kept a close eye on the bread and, when it was suitably brown, you opened the doors and the bread ('automatically') flipped over for toasting on its other side. When those sides were done, you opened the toaster and buttered your achievement.

There was no pop-up system and no warning bell. To my mother, the signal that things had gone too far was usually a cloud of smoke rising to the ceiling. With either the more primitive rack or the 'modern' toaster, my mother managed to frequently blacken and burn. My sisters and I learned to sit at the table and keep an eye on the electrical mechanism when mother was busy at the stove.

I also remember an Orphan Annie plastic shaker with an orange lid — for Ovaltine. I happened to prefer my Ovaltine cold. I put four tablespoons of Ovaltine in the shaker, added milk, firmly caped it, and gave it a solid shaking. The result was a refreshing drink not too unlike a milkshake. Of course, I also had the Orphan Annie secret code ring and a few such other gadgets. My favorite character in the Orphan Annie milieu was the Asp. He was deadly and came in and out of some other special dimension, a good fellow to have on your side.

Model airplane kits were a fashion in my youth. They were not, as they are today, precut and ready for instant assembly. I bought the plans complete with sheets of Balsa wood and did cutting, bending and gluing on my own.

The plane's frame was then covered with thin paper and coated with 'dope.' I don't recall anyone ever sniffing any, or mentioning that it could be done, or getting high on it. Our rumor was that if you put an aspirin or two in a Coke, you could get high. I tried. Nothing happened.

My room, as noted, had a window seat with a lid, providing a nice storage bin. I kept my model planes, during their construction, safely there, until once my tidier older sister opened the lid and deposited several books I had left strewn about — total disaster.

Nevada is both hot and dry. During my prosperous working period at Sprouse-Reitz five and dime, I collected enough money to buy a window cooler which I installed in one of the living room windows that opened out on our front porch. It was of an evaporating water and rotating wick system and quite effective. Since Nevada's summer dryness is extreme, the added moisture in the air was a blessing rather than a curse.

Whistles

An artifact I remember with affection was a Boy Scout pocket knife. It did not have quite as many tool-blades as a Swiss army knife, but it was a multi-purpose wonder nonetheless. I always kept it in my right-hand pocket so as not to damage the living occupant of my left-hand pocket (usually a horned toad). Horned toads could be gathered ad lib at the city dump a couple of miles northeast of Sparks. It was not a felony in those days to carry a knife to school, at least not the kinds of knives we carried around in our pockets.

The dump was also a constant source, rattlesnakes notwithstanding, of useful bits of metal and other artifacts like broken roller skates (for making box scooters), old inner tubes (to be used in the creation and use of rubber guns) and a host of other bits of metal which, if we could not find an immediate use for them, would probably come in handy later on.

My pocket knife was often dedicated to the manufacture of willow whistles. I cannot, after all these years, remember the entire construction. I had to find a nice fresh willow, cut it to a suitable length and then, using the handle of the knife gently rap on the bark until the bark could be slid off the willow wood. Some minor finger cuts almost always resulted.

Then I had to make a V-shaped nick in the wood, and carve out a flat section at the mouthpiece end so air could proceed down the tube. A suitable cut

(I'm vague at this point) had to be made in the bark which was then to be slipped back over the carved willow piece. I know there's more to it than that.

And, quite naturally, the Scout knife was used for whittling and carving. I can't recall why whittling (the cutting down of any available piece of wood to a pile of shavings) was so entertaining, but it was. Often carving had to do with leaving one's initials in tree bark here and there. Or, in one's budding adolescent years, a heart and two sets of initials would do nicely, though they were seldom noted or discovered by the young lady in question.

The Boy's Own Paper

I possessed, to my great good fortune, one thing no other boy in the neighborhood had. It was a large book of bound magazines entitled, 'The Boy's Own Paper.' It was a British production also published in Canada. The book was full of all those things that were of keen and eternal interest to a literate boy. There were stories (probably Wells and others) of hidden valleys in distant lands occupied by undiscovered dinosaurs. There were tales of youthful detection and the incarceration of the villain as a result, with suitable public recognition for good deeds done.

That was a day when good deeds were not limited by potential law suits. Mostly, the book was filled with information about how to build various toys and devices boys happen to find useful (or did then).

I particularly remember one set of instructions for building a movie theatre out of a shoe box, two pegs, paste and linear cuttings from the comic strips.

I learnt much of proper English whilst reading 'The Boy's Own Paper.' Speaking of that, we invented our own telephones. We required two clean cans (no problem with my mother's inability to cook) and a long, strong kite string. We punched a small hole in the bottom of each can, inserted an end of the string in each can, tied a double knot (or more as needed), moved sufficiently apart to pull the string taut and talked to each other. It worked, or at least we thought it did. My idea that we might be able to speak around corners did not, however, work.

Of course we made our own kites, though we did buy the kite string. My box kites were made of thick slats of Balsa and covered with sheets of my model airplane paper and then doped. They were fragile, but could rise at even the least hint of a breeze.

Balsa wood and thinned, doped, tissue paper were better suited for box kites than the regular kind. True, at higher altitudes (I had lots of string) they tended to be torn apart. My tougher (but harder to get airborne) kites were made of regular, crossed wood slats, doped newspaper sheets, and long rag tails. Once up, they could gain awesome altitudes. I always wondered how far they sailed when they broke loose, as they sometimes did. The desert can provide some mighty air currents late of any afternoon.

Perhaps my most valued possession was a top-of-the line Erector set complete with two motors and other special items (among them, a small steam engine). It was a Christmas gift from my father and cost him a goodly sum in those days. I have always suspected, in retrospect, that he made that mighty purchase in order to keep me out of his own construction devices, his tools, and possibly to avoid some of my more inventive surprises around and about the tool shed and the wood shed. It worked well.

I recall building a eight-story elevator with motorized controls that kept my younger sister entertained. Her smaller dolls could be placed in the elevator and, when she threw a small lever, the elevator did what elevators are supposed to do — elevate. I even had a release clutch so that the motor would not burn out when the elevator reached the top or bottom of the tower. And yes, out of the long thin girders I fashioned (according to instructions) a railroad track and a genuine steam engine that moved about with a pleasant puffing. I also built an electric train (the kit came complete with special transformer).

Of all the toys I ever owned, the one I would like to have saved, when my father sold the house, was the Erector set. But he did not know where it had been stored and would not license me any rummaging in the garage attic — which, admittedly, would have required more time than I actually had available.

About Magic

You may not be aware of it, but the first completely successful sex-change operation took place in 1904. I'm referring, of course, to a boy named Tip. Tip had apparently been born a girl, but was immediately transformed by a wicked witch named Mombi into a boy. Tip was about my age (in the book, 'The Land of Oz') when Glinda the Good finally did the dirty work of restoration.

I was shocked! Worse than that! I was stunned. Imagine, a nine year old boy being turned into a girl — a fairy (not inappropriately) princess, no less, named Ozma. I found no comfort in the fact that she was a powerful magician herself and ultimately ruled Oz. Some prices are just too high!

I happened to have two sisters, and our house had only one bathroom, so I was intimately aware of the fact that girls required an enormous number of items of strange 'supportive' clothing and considerable pasting and painting before they could go out there into the world at large. I, on the other hand, required to merely pop into my cords, put on a shirt, socks (sometimes), shoes (except in the summer), wet my hair for combing and toss a bit water on my face to meet any given day or circumstance.

It never took me more than three of four minutes in the bathroom from rising to worldly encounter. The girls, it seemed, spent hours in there doing whatever it was they did. That youthful experience led me in time to the thesis that there must always be at least one more bathroom than the number of women in the house — or a nearby tree screened from public view.

Tip had some wonderful adventures (as a boy) and also a hardy steed to ride, a sawhorse that had been sprinkled with the 'Powder of Life.' It became the fastest and most famous of all the horses of Oz. When Tip was turned into Ozma she had the sawhorse fitted out with gold horseshoes. Tsk! He did well enough roughing it with Tip — that was my opinion at the time.

My favorite magic animal in Oz was 'Kabumpo,' the royal purple elephant owned by Prince Pompadore of the Kingdom of Pumperdink. Like all Oz animals, he spoke. Too, I noted, he had a lot of sense, which Prince Pompadore (early on) did not.

Another favorite Oz animal was 'High Boy.' High Boy was a horse with telescopic legs. He was indeed so skilled at elevating and its reverse that one could get on this 'high horse,' almost at once.

This was an enormous assistance in scouting the territory when trees and other items were blocking the view. And with those long legs, High Boy could really travel. He never quite replaced the Sawhorse for fame, but he was closer to my heart.

My favorite adult male character in Oz was Captain Salt. He had a marvelous pirate ship with balloon sails, and so could not only sail on the water, but through the air when it suited him.

He had a companion called 'Roger the Read Bird.' I always wanted to meet Roger. He sat on the Captain's shoulder (or any of his friends, for that matter) and read aloud from books. Sometimes he could be a bit of an over-cautioning bore, but all in all he meant well. How I envied the American boy Peter who arrived in Oz and traveled with the pirates.

Early Marks

I'm certain our parents regarded the Great Depression with horror, and many people suffered greatly from the long, pinching, episode following Black Friday. I suspect, though it rescued the economy and made work aplenty, WWII was regarded similarly — a mixture of death and opportunity.

But the Great Depression, for those of us who were lucky and were not starved, homeless, or set adrift, provided valuable lessons and benefits.

In the main, we had to create our own amusements and our own toys. Adults had more serious things to do. We made our rubber guns, our box scooters, our push carts, our tree houses, our tunnels and the like. In that, we learned self-sufficiency and the pride of ownership which comes from building with effort.

Our parents, busy with the grimmer doings of economic survival, largely left us to our own devices, based on our solid knowledge that we damned well better do nothing to disgrace the family or the family's good name. Punishment for offense and embarrassment would be, and often was, swift and certain. The rods (or fly swatter handles) were not spared and the child was not spoiled.

Schools and school teachers were always and unquestionably omnipotent. What they said went. Mess up in school, and you were twice straightened out—there and home.

Adults, any of them, spying delinquent behavior, could take such action as they felt the situation required, without the hazard of future lawsuits or accusations of meddling and interference. The telephone, being a fairly common household item, could (and did) permit the prompt relay of information to parents of misbehaving offspring. In due time, there would be hell to pay at home. We knew that and behaved accordingly.

Neighbors were pryingly neighborly. They had a sense of community responsibility for the young well beyond their own immediate families. Children were to be seen and not heard. Children were limited to relatively harmless mischief. Young adults (there were no teenagers at the time), were required to behave themselves as just that, young adults. The neighborly women's network was every bit as efficient as the OSS or the FBI in the uncovering of, or prevention of, crime by children or young adults.

Most important, our schools were small. Sparks High had an enrollment of 350, which meant we were known personally to each and every teacher from the coach to the principal. Troubled folk were easy enough for teachers to spot. One-on-one conferences were frequent. Career advice and counseling was available on a daily basis, not by isolated counselors or distant vice principals, but by folk one met each and every day — the teachers.

To be addressed as 'young man,' or 'young woman,' had about it a certain innate disciplinary force, to say nothing of a set of expectations. 'Kids' were out bleating on the farm and keeping the wild grasses down. Grammar school attendees were identified as 'children.'

The caterers for any school activity were the parents, *not* the cafeteria. We had no cafeteria. We either went home for lunch, time and distance permitting, or brought something to eat in a brown paper bag for lunch in the study hall. The decorators for proms and balls were the students themselves. Cars were scarce, so daters were frequently in pairs or trios. It was regrettably easier to remain virginal in a group.

When our pantry was a little bare I took a small jar of salmon eggs (or a can of worms) and pedaled to the Truckee River and did a bit of afternoon fishing. With skill and/or blind luck, there would be four or five rainbow trout for dinner. Now that was a real contribution to the welfare of the family.

The Great Depression left its marks on its generation of young: creativity, individuality, self-sufficiency, realistic expectations, demands made not *by* us, but *of* us, a work ethic, if only work could be found, and a sense of contribution to the family, or the community, or the school, and ultimately the nation.

Malnutrition and not obesity, was the problem for the young and their elders. Would be Caesars were kept suitably wary. Almost all, we had a lean and hungry look.

Mr. Lewis

When I was in high school, Mr. Lewis, a retired farmer of some 86 or 87 years, moved in with his daughter and family across the street.

They also owned a large, empty, corner lot (where we fellows played baseball) on the corner next to their house.

Old habits are hard to discard, so every spring Mr. Lewis brought in a team of horses from his ranch (presumably now operated by other members of the family), plowed the lot and planted vegetables. Some of his crops were different than our own, so we purchased seasonally what extras we wanted from him, as did others in our neighborhood.

He had one aggravation however. In the center of the empty lot was a giant cottonwood tree which, it was said, plagued Mr. Lewis because it interfered, roots and all, with his plowing and his crops.

Eventually, he was told that he had a bad heart and that his gardening days were over. This was shortly after I left home for the Navy.

When I got back, the cottonwood tree was gone and the empty garden-lot was now occupied by a new brick house.

I was told that, knowing he could no longer farm, even on a miniature basis, the old man took a double-bladed ax, felled the mighty cottonwood precisely where he wanted it, and dropped dead as a result of his effort, the double-bladed ax still in hand.

The other cottonwood in front of the original house was removed some years later at great expense.

That's the tale and I like the telling of it.

Theatres

Reno had one large and elegant theatre, the Majestic, and two smaller and less grand ones, the Granada and the Wigwam. These latter two were cheaper too, and the Wigwam had the advantage of a restaurant directly across the street named the 'Wigwam Café'' The café had a specialty — hot apple pie, an after-theatre treat of no small measure.

Sparks, on the other hand, had a theatre of a most primitive sort. I can remember only one silent movie shown there; 'The Gold Rush.' I have a more vivid memory of the introduction of movie sound with the showing of the 'The Jazz Singer.'

The movie house was a wooden structure that in the wee hours of one morning burnt to the ground. It was replaced by another emergency 'theatre' in a lesser building. I remember walls lined with sacking and sack curtains at the entrance to keep out the light and wooden benches to sit on. This made the people in Sparks intemperate, and there was a demand for something better.

Eventually, Mr. Cook, a tall rather elegant gentleman with silver hair, arrived in town, bought out the other fellow and, clever man, made some kind of financial deal with the City of Sparks wherein they would help him build an entirely new and 'modern' theatre. It would be less grand than Reno's Majestic but a bit grander than either the Granada or the Wigwam. We anxiously watched its construction and attended its glorious opening, awed by the comfortable seats, and bigger screen, and elegant maroon carpeting. There were gilded pillars and other luxuries too.

Mr. Cook was fond of children and set up all manner of fun arrangements for Saturday and Sunday matinees. There were drawings of ticket stubs after each show and prizes awarded. The grand prize, one time, was an airplane tied with a cable to a central post that actually could be flown in an eight-foot circle. We were allowed to stand in line, after the movie, and fly it. I think it was Claud Calendar who finally (oh envious greed on the part of the rest of us) won the prize. He gained a sudden spurt of friends as a result. Alas, I bought one of those machines when my daughters were but girls. They were not impressed. I played with it a while and gave it to Doug Rigg, a neighborhood lad who had a sense of appreciation.

The Saturday serial that scared me the most was a series called 'Tarzan and the Green Goddess.' Each episode ended with Tarzan falling off a cliff, or being attacked by an alligator, or being mobbed by a horde of spear-armed natives.

One of the lesser fellows in Tarzan's party, under attack by a mighty native mob, unpacked a secret suitcase which contained a machine gun and chopped down the lot. We gloried in the slaughter.

My second favorite serial was 'Flash Gordon.' I found Ming the Merciless really scary. Why, the man even mistreated his attractive daughter. There were two women fighting for Flash's attention. We ignored them both!

I have a very clear memory of attending a Saturday matinee (mid-winter) to see a movie called 'Frankenstein.' My mistake was that I had forgotten the sun was going to have been long set when I came out of the theatre to wend my way home some seven blocks. It was a frightening journey I can tell you. Who knew in which bush the monster lurked?

And did I think of Count Dracula? Well, even then, I found Bela Lugosi too much the ham. The trick of flashing a light across his eyes did not make him that much scarier either. Much later Christopher Lee became a seriously frightening vampire — he was tall, sinister, tinted faintly green and, newly sated, his eyes always filled with blood.

The original 'King Kong' was first class and, compared to a recent remake, still the best. The same can be said for 'The Bride of Frankenstein,' one of those rare occasions (as with the Godfather) when the sequel was better than the original. The original 'Thing,' mocks the later gorier and bloody sequel. I grew up in an era when the hero *didn't* have more beautiful hair than the heroine, and it was the villains who didn't shave.

In later perspective, there was one thing that came to my attention. All the villains in our serials wore hats. They had marvelous fist fights with the hero. Oddly, those bad guys never lost a hat in a fight, however violent and however gymnastic. Why, they could fall thirty feet off a cliff, roll another hundred yards, and rise to fight again, hats still firmly in place. And that, before instant glue!

To re-view these Saturday serials as adults should never be done. The phony rockets and guide wires and wavering flames are now too plain. The absence of any plot seemed obvious. All of which may explain the success of 'Star Wars' — our old serials revamped, revised, and developed with new techniques to the point of adult believability.

Another Age

There was a time when Halloween products began to be sold only in October, Thanksgiving sales began immediately after Halloween, and Christmas stocks, decorations and sales did not begin until Thanksgiving was safely stuffed away.

Basketball season did not begin until football season was duly over and baseball did not begin until the basketball games were all wrapped up. That is, sports were genuinely seasonal with a pleasant interlude during the summer months.

I had sisters and Princesses Elizabeth and Margaret Rose arrived in the form of paper dolls.

Any boy who was a boy had a pocket knife. Any scout who was a scout had a scout knife. The rich kids carried a Swiss Army knife, that epitome of tool consolidation.

Old men sat around and whittled and abjured running for public office.

The mentally ill were housed in mental institutions under medical supervision and normally did not bathe in the public fountains, or slumber in the public library. We had no public fountains, and Mr. Carnegie was only beginning to supply the libraries.

Girls wore skirts and boys wore pants.

Fraternity and sorority houses ringed almost any campus — the frats were synonymous with Friday beer busts and the sororities were virtual, weekend, virginal nunneries.

The cameraman discretely contemplated nearby scenery in lieu of focusing on any actual sexual encounter.

I remember what a 'cat's whisker' was and how it related to broadcasting. Dare I mention a crystal set?

The farm kids wore overalls to school, over their pants only in the winter. Other seasons the pants were dispensed with. It was cooler that way.

Summer school had to do with religious training and the schools were either Mormon or Catholic. Protestant youths frequently went Scot free. Oh to be a Protestant when summer's here!

Juvenile sex was mostly dream and idle speculation.

I wanted to be a champion, so I ate Wheaties for breakfast.

I had an Orphan Annie code ring and I knew how to use it. And, lucky me, I had an Orphan Annie Ovaltine shaker. I was familiar with Buck Rogers and knew about his old foe Killer Kane. Ardella did not interest me as I was not yet pubescent.

I had to open the grocery store door on my own. Also it was the same with the garage door.

I knew the Shadow knew. Does anyone remember Lamont Cranston?

The relationship between Batman and Robin was not suspect.

Anyone who had reached 5' 10' was destined to be a basketball center.

Girls played 'Jacks' or 'Jump Rope.' Boys played 'Mumble Peg.'

A vacant lot, a ball and a bat were all that was required for baseball. There was no Little League. Girls played softball. Boys played hardball.

More Games

Nevada is mostly a high plateau on the Western edge of the Great American Desert, the long west/east stretch of sand and alkali is wrinkled from Sparks to Wendover on the state's eastern edge by a series of north/south, ridges and hills. They are frequently snow-capped in the winter. Here and there hide dales and dells parenthesized in green. But they are rare.

Nevada had teenages (not teenagers) long before the latter invention became popular. A teenage was (and still is for all I know) a low fence of anchored sage brush (in Nevada anyway). It's a British term, to be found in the O.E.D. but they use the word 'brush' as an unqualified noun.

Once you get a bit east of Sparks and beyond the shadow of the high Sierras, you encounter a wind that never ceases. It ranges from a whisper in the eaves to high-pitched screaming at the intruding building corners when weather's afloat, so the teenages are often necessary to prevent dunes from overpowering the scarce farm and range lands.

The fences are sometimes re-enforced by a further collection of queued tumbleweeds. It is the tumbleweeds that are of interest here because they were involved in a game most of you have never played. Unimaginatively, we called the game 'tumbleweeds.' When the weeds had finished their growth, dried out, and gotten free to roll about, we would round up some of them ranging in size from bigger than a basketball to smaller than a medicine ball. We would also gather four to five foot sturdy sticks (discarded broom or mop handles were perfect) and then, and only then, could the game begin — hockey without the puck and sans the skates and ice.

The object of the game was to be able to drive your tumbleweed to some selected goal (a telephone pole or a lamp post, most likely) in the enemy's territory and prevent a similar drive toward a similar artifact in your own. It would have been an easy sport except for Nevada's eternal winds which had a habit of interfering with the best-laid plans of the players. The dried weeds were always light and susceptible to major influence by any passing breeze. This made a true contest of it — fighting off the opposition and planning for Mamma Nature's unpredictable interferences in the game.

Given the height of the tumbleweeds, shins were much more likely than ankles to be damaged by over-enthusiastic opposition.

We shrugged such incidents aside. I cannot recall a single clash with the sticks as in our 'modern' hockey games. We got dusty. We got knocked down frequently. We swore a bit now and then at some inadvertent injury. But we never exploded into violence and rage. It was a sport, you see, and sportsmanship (devoid of the pressures of heady money) still reigned. Coaches did give a damn about losing gracefully in those days. Alas, they have no current compunction, and one wonders how much that has to do with the demeaned and discontented, the losers, arriving at the school with fully loaded pistols in search of deadly vengeance for past slights both real and imagined.

Due to our near location to the lower regions of the Sierras, we had another game of which I seldom hear these days. We called it 'body rafting.' We found a fast-running, icy, mountain stream and rode it feet first and on our backs wherever it would take us. The streams were not only fast and icy, but rock-ridden, and we knew intuitively that our butts were softer than our heads and could endure a good deal more punishment. And, naturally, we wanted to protect another vital (well, maybe not yet) area from hard blows. At those tender ages, we all had rubber bodies. I have come to believe modern anatomy has shifted, the heads are now soft and buttocks hard, so the game may not be currently popular for good reason.

Cursed Technology

In the later 1930's, cap pistols became popular. But you had to purchase the pistol and the caps (and we never had enough caps). The 'bang' was very realistic, but one's actual aiming skill was not tested. Ergo, lots of arguments about who was dead and who was not. With the rubber gun, when you got hit, you got hit, and everyone knew it.

Old inner tubes had other uses, perhaps more dangerous than rubber guns. I'm referring to that instrument which any 'real' boy carried around in his back pocket — a slingshot. This was a Y-shaped piece of a tree branch with a strip of thin-cut inner tube (usually with the middle cut larger than the rest to form a pouch to hold a pebble. The two ends of the tube strip overlapped the tops of the forks of the branch and were firmly tied down with several 'winds' of string or wire.

We were instructed not to 'shoot' at each other, but the occasional bird or stray rabbit was an acceptable target. Mostly, the critters were quite safe! We had terrible aim. On occasion a window shattered, and there was 'hell to pay.' There were a lot of sling shots being toted around at our grammar school and later, junior high, but I don't remember them coming out of back pockets very often. They were given up, a few years later, for another object which, through lack of any use, left a ring on one side or the other of one's wallet. The telltale ring was the important thing!

We never used the term 'macho' in those days. But we did refer to the more daring (and usually older set) as 'real guys' (as versus the rest of us who were only dreamers).

Simpler Times

Sparks, Nevada, when I was little, had not yet had a long acquaintance with electricity, so the power failed frequently, and we were stocked with kerosene lamps. We used them enough to 'smoke up' the glass chimneys. Since my hands were small, I was often given a clean cloth and instructed to wipe the soot out of the chimneys and also trim the wicks. I always got dirty doing that, which always resulted in a need to wash my hands thoroughly (and while I was at it, behind my ears) which is one of the things small boys do not have high on their popularity list of things to do.

I don't know just why it was assumed that dirt would quickly collect behind one's ears, but washing behind them was something of a standing order. My own ears, like those of Bing Crosby, did not seem to be positioned close enough to my head to collect anything of significance. As a matter of cold fact, I could not, like other people, place a pencil behind either of my ears and expect it to remain there. This misfortune holds true yet.

Someone mentioned sneakers the other day, particularly Keds. I had them too. They were called 'gym shoes' and did not meet with my mother's approval for regular wear. Apparently, they carried, in due course and with proper neglect, a powerful odor of their own. This aroma could not match, however, the smell of a gym towel finally returned home at the end of a semester when one was required to clean out and empty his locker and carry home any number of items that had been lost for at least two months or more.

Dead and dried horned toads were not to be returned home, if I remember my instructions correctly. Lockers were indoors and marched down long halls in those days. The sounds of lockers opening and slamming shut at the beginning and ending of each class has probably disappeared from the student world. In fact, I gather lockers are now considered (what with bombs and all) a threat to the safety of the students, the teachers, the administrators and the janitors.

Lockers may make a come back, though, for the health folk have announced that shoulder bags and knapsacks have been deforming the younger children of the land and may require to be banned. We carried our books (those that we felt we needed to take home (a rare event) to and fro bound together with an old belt. They were, during some of our altercations on the school grounds, used with the effectiveness of a mace. The mayhem went unnoticed (children were expected to have to endure one or more minor hazards in those days) and the belting of books was never banned.

Lockers were not common in grammar school. We had a single room and desks with lids on them and provision for ink wells. Just above the desktop hinges, I recall small grooves for pens and pencils. There was also something of a sense of historic continuity, since most of the desks contained the carved initials of those who had gone before. This made for rough writing surfaces, but no one seemed too concerned about it. Once in a rare while, we would return to school after a long, pleasant summer and discover that the desktops had all been sanded and varnished. This purity of condition did not last all that long.

No boy I knew in Sparks ever traveled without his pocket knife. One boy who actually was from Switzerland, had a genuine Swiss army knife which was quite differently equipped than any sold in America under that name. The official Boy Scout knife (I had one of those too) was a simpler device. But then, the Boy Scouts were a simpler group.

There were no girls in the Boy Scouts then, nor were there any boys in the Girl Scouts. There were no coed locker rooms or gym classes or dorms or any of that type of thing. The school authorities (particularly as puberty arrived on the scene) wisely felt casual intermingling was dangerous enough on its own without any encouragement. It was not that much of a problem because we were sufficiently retarded that girls did not enter into our calculations until about the sophomore year in high school. It was then that the age of reason hit the dust never to return. We were not, happily, probed or pushed into 'relationships' before our time. Nor were the authorities saddled by outside interferences on any scale comparable with those today. Teachers and principals were assumed to know what they were about, and it was a rare event indeed that caused any direct parental inquiries.

We rarely reported any of our school 'violations' to our parents and the teachers largely (again with the exception of cases of outright mayhem) kept their own counsel.

We were, prior to puberty, mostly wary of girls. They clearly did not like little boys (and the feelings were often mutual) and they 'tattled' (sisters in particular). Today girls of all ages don't tattle, they insist on the legal re-enforcement of their rights which seem to be expanding at an alarming rate. I can't speak for how it was for girls in an earlier day, but it was definitely easier for boys who, we are now told, are lately being persecuted ad lib, and it is damaging them somehow. I doubt it. As boys we always thought we were being persecuted (too noisy, too active, too irreverent, too vulgar) and, as Ripley (from Aliens) suggested, we dealt with it even though not named Hudson. I could be wrong, but I don't think girls then, based on the current cacophony, were any unhappier than they claim to be now.

Old Jones

I was taught to be polite to my elders, so I called the old gentleman Mr. Jones. He was thought to be somewhat dotty (which I doubted) and hence was called 'Old Jones,' by his railroad colleagues who had not yet reached their own late age and were not retired or in the habit of talking to themselves. Personally, I thought Mr. Jones had much to mutter about.

I liked him. He had an old 1928 Dodge sedan and was very kind in letting me sit in it (parked on the road by the side of his house which was on the corner) and pretend to drive and work my way through the odd gear shift (somewhat the reverse of most). Then, in 1936, he bought a brand new Plymouth sedan, one of the first of the cars to have an all steel top as versus the old tarred canvas mid-section. He let me play in the new car too, though Mrs. Jones often screamed her objection through the window, 'Get that boy out of our new car!'

Mr. Jones would wink at me and say, 'Pay her no mind, son. She barks a lot more than she bites. Have your fun.' I did.

The following year, July, he let me help him put a new shingle roof on his house. I thoroughly enjoyed myself even though working on the roof was a very hot experience. My dad, coming home from the railroad that way one day, mentioned that Mr. Jones (the 'old fool') was butting the shingles together instead of leaving a crack between shingles for expansion.

'First rain,' Dad said, 'the roof will buckle and leak. There should be a nail-width between each shingle at the very least. You might want to mention that.'

I pointed out the fact to Mr. Jones, but he said it was easier to butt the shingles against each other and they would shrink during the summer in any event. I conferred with Dad. He said the shingles would not shrink very much, if at all, since they probably had been in the Nevada lumber yard a while and would have thoroughly dried out already.

'Just go ahead,' he said, 'and put a nail's width between the shingles you install, the old fool won't notice anyway.' So that's what I did.

It really did not matter anyway, because Mr. Jones died of pneumonia shortly after Christmas the following winter, and I know why! He had been tossed out of the bedroom years earlier by Mrs. Jones who was at least 20 years his junior.

She claimed he snored and so he was forced to sleep on the back porch which was screened only. Well, the screening was of the 'glazed' type. That is the pores were sealed by something akin to clear plastic to keep out the rain and snow. But it certainly did not keep out the cold, and Nevada winters can get very cold indeed.

My bones are creaky enough in my early eighties even waking up in a warm house. I shudder at the thought of sleeping on an ice-cold Nevada porch in the middle of a hard winter. The winter Mr. Jones got pneumonia and died was one of Nevada's record cold winters with a lot of snow and temperatures down near zero at night. There was plenty of wind that winter too, though no one worked out a 'wind chill factor,' in those distant days.

Whenever Mrs. Jones wanted Mr. Jones to come in for lunch or dinner (I know nothing of breakfast), she would scream out into the yard, 'come and eat you old fool!' I did not think that was very nice of her, but apparently it was her habit. I did not like Mrs. Jones on that account, among others.

After Mr. Jones died, I used to jump over Mrs. Jones's hedge which separated her house from the immediate neighbor. Several of my friends, under my direction, would do likewise. We did not often clear the hedge top. This always brought Mrs. Jones out to her front porch screaming about our ruining her hedge, and that we would be duly reported. We were.

My mother inquired about it. I said we did no serious damage and besides, we did not like Mrs. Jones as she had been mean to Mr. Jones and I thought that's why he died.

'It's like the story of the poor little match girl,' I opined.

That silenced my mother, and I never received any further static at home.

Those who seek revenge often find themselves with a mouthful of ashes. Our revenge must not have been serious, as we usually just wound up with a shoe full of hedge leaves.

Sacred Objects

My dad's railroad watch was a sacred object which, when not in his watch pocket, braided leather fob included, rested on an unassailable place, the top of his dresser. In our early days, we could not reach there. In our taller days, we knew better than to try.

When Dad was home, another object rested safe and secure on the dresser top, his railroad lantern. It was, in the first instance, a kerosene lantern (the fuel for which was often called 'coal oil'). Later, it was an electric affair which was fueled by a large six-volt battery. It had two bulbs installed and a switch to shift from one to the other, 'a safety factor,' such that if one bulb burned out, there was a ready reserve.

When the glow of the bulbs grew dim, the battery was changed. The old battery was placed in a similar railroad lantern which hung on a hook in the sun porch in case of a power failure (not as frequent then as in the earlier days). Battery replacement was a linear affair; railroad lantern to porch lantern to garbage pail.

When Dad moved from freight brakeman or freight conductor to passenger trains, he went from wearing blue overalls to a uniform. At that time, the braided leather watch fob was exchanged for a sturdy gold one.

It was interesting that, in Sparks at least, the engineers wore striped overalls and the freight brakemen and conductors wore solid blue overalls. It never occurred to me to ask why, so I do not know whether that was a self-imposed distinction made by the trainmen themselves or forced upon them from on high. Nor do I know, for that matter, whether the work-clothes distinction was local or applied over a large geographic area.

Dad's black, dome-topped, lunch box was also of a sacred nature; not a toy, not to be played with, not to be bothered. And even more so, the Thermos bottle that clamped inside the high-topped lid. It was explained to us that Thermos bottles were expensive and of a delicate nature due to their glass linings (which created the vacuum which kept the contents warm or cold as the case might be) and were to be carefully treated.

Both the lunch box and the Thermos bottle did not rest on Dad's dresser but on a special high, shelf in the pantry. That shelf too, was sacred.

There were two other untouchables, one in the house and the other in the garage. We had a wood/coal stove in both the kitchen and the living room. Beside the kitchen stove, high up on the left wall, was a matchbox container. We used large wooden matches in those days for the starting of fires in either stove. 'Children do not play with matches,' was an eleventh Commandment in our house and was enforced in the first instance by a sharp slap across the hand and on any repeated instance with the swift and stinging justice of the wire handle of the flyswatter across the rump.

Before the electric lanterns arrived, the metal can containing the 'coal oil' for Dad's lanterns resided on the workbench in the tool shed along with a spare lantern. Any attempt at investigating (or playing) with either brought a sharp rap on the forehead with the extended middle knuckle of Dad's right hand. It stung, but was never administered with such force as to cause brain damage.

When Dad had been 'bumped' to the 'extra board' by a senior employee, he often used his extra time off to re-wick, clean the glass chimney, and see to the proper fueling of his regular lantern and the spare in the garage. He might even take the time to repaint the exterior of his lunch box when it had been chipped or dented.

Dad's disciplinary equipment, the extended knuckle, was portable and always available when required. The flyswatter handle, my mother's favorite weapon, sat on top of the bun warmers over the kitchen range where it would 'be handy.'.

As far as I know, those bun warmers never warmed buns. They were the storage bins for the most frequently used pots and pans.

The odd thing about all this is that we did not think ourselves abused either by being required to avoid certain tools or this or that shelf, or by the arrival of the occasional disciplinary rap on the forehead, or fly swatter across the rump. Today, I suppose, my parents would be charged with all manner of 'abuses' by prying, self-righteous, meddling neighbors. At that earlier date, no such meddling would have been thought of; more likely, there would have been nods of approval.

As far as I know, the English poet, Samuel Butler's, lyric advice, 'Love is a boy, by poets styled. Then spare the rod, and spoil the child,' was followed. Or maybe the source of parental insurance came from the original austere Biblical admonition in Proverbs: 'Spare the rod and spoil the child.' Whatever the source, they believed it, and acted on it!

Schools

When I was attending to such matters (circa the early 1930s) Sparks, Nevada, not unlike Caesar's Gaul, was divided into three parts - - at least as far as grammar schools were concerned. The main grammar school (Robert Mitchell, grades K-6) was located somewhat in the center of town. On the eastern edge was the Mary Lee Nichols grammar school (K-3) and at the western edge, the Kate Smith Grammar school (K-3). I do not know who Mary Lee and Kate were, or why they had the small schools named after them. Maybe they had been great teachers of the past, or had financed the erection of the buildings in question? Hard to say, and I never inquired.

Dwight Diltz was the Principal of the Robert Mitchell Grammar school, and I presume had vice principals running the other two smaller schools. Since I was originally located somewhat centrally in Sparks, I attended the Robert Mitchell School from grades K-6. When we did move to the west side of town, I was already beyond the third grade so not eligible to attend the Kate Smith school which was just a block or two from our house.

Well, Kindergarten for but a day. I found myself there on the first day of school but since I could already read and write, I took myself to the first grade after morning recess. After a demonstration of my reading ability, and the concurrence of Principal Diltz, I was allowed to remain in the first grade and thus became the class dwarf for the rest of my school career in Sparks. This was not necessarily a happy circumstance. Too, because most school work came rather easily to me, I was also often unpopular on that account, but that's life in the pencil sharpener factory.

In those more primitive and less parent-directed days, going back to school was an ambivalent experience, a mixture of curiosity and despair. It also involved having to wear shoes again, and finding that the old shoes no longer fitted, and the new ones either pinched or squeaked for a good while. Tennis shoes (Keds, as they were called in those days) were frowned upon except for P. E. classes because they tended to stink after a while. Of course, gym towels also suffered a similar fate since they tended to reside in our gym locker (parental nagging notwithstanding) for a full semester before we were forced to empty our lockers.

The usual debris hauled out of lockers at the end of the term included a pair or two of old socks which could well have been used as weapons of mass destruction in subways or other restricted places except for the fact we did not have any.

Large amounts of scrap paper (provided by the school) also had to be thrown out, even if in the form of worn-out paper airplanes. I have already mentioned the gym towels from the locker room in the gym along with gym suits and other male equipment inclined to have gone downright moldy.

For the main school lockers (always in the halls out of the weather and locked with a combination lock), the discovery of library books long unreturned was not uncommon. There were so many of those, special tables were usually set up in the halls for the return with no questions asked. The same held true for any purloined collections of pens, pencils, and tablets (provided free by the school).

In my grammar years, returning to school often involved the purchase of a 'pencil box,' which was much more than that, since it always had fascinating things in it like a compass (of the circle-making kind), and a protractor, and a small pencil sharpener, etc. One could get the Prince Valiant or Batman or Robin Hood variety according to heroic predilection.

My early summers were ruined by my being forced to attend half-day Catholic summer classes at the Nichols school, which was a good mile or so away. But it did bring about a somewhat infamous occasion when Sister Teresa had been giving us a vivid description of Satan, and I had later wandered off into the hall and encountered Old Nick himself; that is, he was tall, thin, and dressed in red, though he was, at the moment, minus horns and tail. I advised him of Sister Teresa's general animosity and suggested he had best depart. Alas, it was Bishop Gorman visiting the school, and he was much amused when I asked if his red beanie was covering his horns, and did he have his tail tucked away in his robe? I was much abashed by his remembrance and telling of the tale a few years later at my confirmation.

Such is fame.

Surprises from Dad

Speaking of Dad, and I have been, he was Canadian, which meant that, among other things, he was proficient at ice skating, skiing, and hockey. It seemed to have come naturally to him, more so than his brothers. When we were little, he would skate with us on the occasional frozen pond, usually in his overalls, but no matter. He could do a reasonable number of maneuvers commonly the property of professional skaters. I, for one, had all I could do to stand up and skate straight, and then bemoan the weakness of my ankles at the end of the day. None of my friends, if I remember correctly, skated well enough for a game of hockey. Or I don't remember any. We had clamp-on skates rather than shoe skates, so that may have been the major part of the problem.

But Dad hit his peak of surprises, as I recall, in his forties or fifties when we had gone to Mr. Rose with some other families to watch the skiers. The lodge at Mt. Rose featured one of the larger ski jumps in the area, not quite Olympic size, but long and steep enough to near qualify.

Watching a while, Dad decided that there had been severer jumps in Canada and, against the protests of my mother and two of our neighborhood friends, he mentioned he thought he might give it a try. So off he went up the lift to the top of the jump and there he managed to persuade one of the younger men to loan him both his boots and his skis.

In due course, in his best suit, and holding tightly with one hand to his best hat, down the jump he came, sailed off into the broad blue yonder and landed without so much as a teeter.

Satisfied, he returned the boots and skis and gave a small bow to all and sundry. The startled crowd had treated him to a heady round of applause.

He was also the only one of his nine brothers who had been taught to play the piano. We had the black twin version of the Virginia City rosewood piano in our house; it came with the place because it was, from the former owner's point of view, 'too heavy and too expensive' to move. I don't know whether Dad paid him extra for the piano or not. The matter never came up.

Of many a quiet evening, even after we got the radio, Dad would sit down, complain of being rusty, and play. He preferred the marches of Mr. Sousa, but also had some other favorites. I remember only one of them: 'The Black Hawk.' Was that a march or waltz? I honestly can't remember. Anyway, it seemed to be a fairly peppy piece.

Liberace stopped by during one of the times of his Reno performances and tried to buy the piano. This enchanted my mother much more than my father, but he refused to sell it as he had promised it to the little girl next door if and when he moved. He kept his promise, much to my relief, when he sold the house and disposed of its contents to all and sundry.

I skied from time to time, but not a lot. Still, I gifted my children with something of an equivalent surprise when we went water skiing.

On one occasional a large boat came by making a very deep wake behind which I momentarily disappeared. The girls cheered when I popped up over the crest in due course, still on the skis. Water skiing, by the way, is much easier than snow skiing, even to the point of not having to encounter the occasional tree, as I sometimes did on the Sierra slopes.

It is often as much a surprise to one's children that their parents can actually do anything other than nag, as it is to college students that, on weekends, the professors do not fall between some dusty book covers to only reappear again on Monday.

Tea and Sympathy

I have never ever had to wonder how it was the people of a small island (Britain) managed to dominate one fourth of the globe. It was, in my opinion, due entirely to tea; first the search for it and second, the habitual drinking of it.

My mother's father was Chief Gamekeeper for Lord Lovat (of Scotland). Accordingly, when Lovat's hunting parties were not aboard (which was most of the time), my grandfather was lord of the manor, which meant that my mother only saw a kitchen rarely, and knew absolutely nothing about how food got cooked or arrived at the table, with one sterling exception. She did know how to make and serve tea in the British tradition. Aristocratic young ladies had at least that much domestic training.

Come hell, high water, war or weather, my mother always had tea at approximately four o'clock of every afternoon. It had, in times of stress, she used to say, a calming influence and brought respite and perspective, and that, dear hearts, is the British secret.

My father, one of nine boys (with one lone sister), and one of the youngest, found himself assigned to work in the kitchen. Accordingly, he learned to cook moderately well and so, in spite of my mother's inadequacies in that respect, we managed to survive. Too, it was not long before my sisters and I decided, in our own self defense, to learn to cook, mostly from watching Dad.

Ultimately, my mother learned to manage roast beef with Yorkshire pudding, an excellent leg of lamb, a tasty ham, and the Christmas turkey. But once the main meal was over, what to do with leftovers defeated her, and she resorted to reheating things in the frying pan.

It was a good while before I learned that heartburn was not an automatic aftermath of the ordinary daily dinner.

I managed to survive by a keen knowledge of the neighborhood and a certain skill at getting invited in for dinner or snacks. I would not want to insist that my closer friends just happened to have mothers who were excellent cooks and were chosen on that account alone, but looking back, that may have been a matter of serious weight.

Mrs. Lightfoot made the best candies and cookies in town. Every Christmas we were presented with a wonderful box of her best efforts. We looked forward to that. She also made other tasty dishes, such as casseroles, and my friend Don and I often decided I should stay for dinner so we could play afterward.

Mrs. Ball baked fresh bread every Thursday and always made a most excellent apple butter to go along with the warm bread and butter. I could frequently skip dinner entirely by going off to play with the other Donald at just about two on any afternoon.

Mrs. Barbieri concocted wonderful doughy pillows filled with tasty meats and spices. They were called ravioli. She also used wine in her salad dressings, which I thought was very daring of her.

Mrs. Zenclusen, a true farm wife, created all manner of good things which would, these days, be called German fare. Her pastries were particularly tasty as I remember. All her dinner dishes had strange names and were marvelously flavorful and edible.

I had a mental map of the town and knew all the better invitational eating places such that I could manage to 'eat out' when Mother was doing business with just the frying pan. Have you ever tried a once boiled and now fried Brussels sprout? Don't!

Happily, a Mr. Thorsen lived next door to us. He was a professional baker who, at home, constructed wonderful wedding cakes to enhance his income. He also made pies for 25 cents which could be purchased by his neighbors. My dad could make pies that were tasty, but the crusts (to be kind) could have well been used to resole shoes. Mr. Thorsen's crusts really would melt in your mouth. As often as I could, I would persuade Mother to part with a quarter so we could have a Thorsen pie.

But, as I said, tea was quite another matter. I learned how to be a master at the brewing. First, one had to have a proper earthenware pot. Said pot had to be rinsed with boiling water before any attempt at making tea. The pot, suitably heated and steeped a while, could then be drained, the pinches of black tea added, the boiling water poured, the next steeping timed to a gnat's tick, and then the tea served. For those of a weaker character, cream and sugar could be added. Mother preferred her tea with just 'a touch' of sugar. She was not into the squeeze-of-lemon group, though slices of lemon were often available for those who preferred their tea that way. The tea, as noted, was not green (that was for the delicate Chinese), but black, a critical difference. When available, scones or chilled cucumber sandwiches (in hot weather) would accompany the tea. Iced tea, even in the heat of the tropics or the jungle, was considered barbaric.

My mother always preferred my bachelor visits to my sisters' visits (what with husbands and children and all), because she could say, 'Oh good, it's you. Go buy hamburgers, and I will put on the tea pot.' It was a much the simpler way to handle things; the burgers for substance, the tea for character.

WWII destroyed my tea habit. It was replaced by Navy coffee so powerful there was not a chance in hell one would or could fall asleep on watch. The Navy coffee pots were thickly lined with years of accumulated coffee stain and other debris. The coffee was served hot and black. If you could not drink it, you could at least warm your hands by firmly gripping the mug.

Next time the media try to send you into a panic, stop! Make some tea! Drink tea and you will see! Today the teacup! Tomorrow the world!

The Tool Maker

Dad had been a machinist before he became a railroad brakeman. He had a goodly supply of expensive tools, and we must remember, it was the time of the Great Depression. Naturally, I wanted a set of such excellent tools myself. At the age of eight or nine, I could not afford them. What would be a wise solution? Do what I'd read about in the matter of casting lead toy soldiers. Get about creating molds.

I spent a happy period (Dad was often gone on the RR for a week or more at a time) using mill blocks to make tool molds. Luckily, there was always a bag or two of cement in the shed since Dad was about the business of converting the wooden back stoop to a concrete one.

When I had my tool molds done, I filled the bottom half with the cement, carefully placed the tool in question (including some very expensive calipers), inserted some wax paper around the tool edges, and then poured cement on top. Concrete molds would soon follow. I had the wit to use pegs to keep holes for the future pouring of metal, though which metal, and how I was to come by it and melt it, had yet to be decided.

There was one serious oversight, however. Well, one can't think of everything. I did not provide for the fact that the cement (a thin mixture) would get under and mingle with the finer features of the tools in question, leaving the wax paper insufficient for proper separation. Dad came home to find a small fortune of his best devices, solidly implanted in concrete blocks, but, mind you, very neatly stacked near his workbench.

Chisel and hammer in hand, he salvaged what he could. But some tools are delicate and wet cement takes time to turn to concrete and wet makes rust, and weight, for the more delicate instruments, can warp beyond usability. It took Dad a good while even to get started. He gave up the expression 'Sam Hill' (insisted upon my mother in lieu of other expletives) and did a great deal of muttering in violent railroad language.

I had never seen my father that angry (not even over the elephant trap or my Egyptian doings with tool shed and wood shed doors), and my sister agrees.

Naturally, I stayed my distance. Much later, when he was off on the road again, I chipped out what he had not, though not skillfully. This may explain why, when my mother died and he later sold the house, he insisted the new owner should have his tools. I was lucky to get away with Grandfather's prize hammer.

One time, when I was much older, I asked him if he was using a set of pipe cutters and threaders which I had my eye on. 'No. But you can buy your own damned tools,' he said sharply.

Perhaps, he was justified. Had he been less tolerant in his younger years, and mine, I would not have been around.

The Canter Sisters

The Canter sisters were not made of sugar and spice and everything nice. Nor did they wear skirts, blouses and saddle shoes. Rather, the two girls, about a year apart in age, wore Levis, red checkered shirts and boots. Their hair was cut suitably short to match their apparel. They also owned and rode a Harley motorcycle, usually with something bordering on reckless abandon, or so it was often reported.

They were in high school, and I was just beginning junior high. Accordingly, they seemed to be incredibly adult and enormously interesting.

I was given a ride on the Harley once, by the older sister. It was both thrilling and scary. I did not report the adventure to my parents.

My dad mentioned, when I asked him once, that the girls were 'hard.' My mother replied to a similar question that they were 'coarse.' I suppose they were. But they seemed adventurous and attractive insofar as they were not gossipy or girlish which, at the beginning of junior high is not necessarily a bad thing in the consideration of boys.

Too, the sisters had one other fascinating advantage. They owned an eagle which they kept in a very large cage behind their home which just happened to be, would you not know, on the wrong side of the Sparks railroad tracks. The bird was large, but not as huge as an eagle I once saw in the wild. The girls brought him out of his cage from time to time on an extended leash and handled him with heavy leather work gloves. Equipped with the gloves, I was permitted to hold him once and he weighed a good deal more than I expected. I was told he would bite so to keep him at arms length. It seemed to me that my arms were not quite the length I would have preferred them to be, but I managed to hold him un-bitten.

I never knew and never inquired about how the girls were regarded in high school as to whether they were 'easy' or not. That was not, at the time, of any serious interest in my world. They did play baseball with some of the older fellows and that seemed appropriate.

The two girls did not make high school graduation. They were particularly fond of tandem (the younger girl behind the older) high speed doings on the road to Mt. Rose, one of the routes to Lake Tahoe. In the late Fall the mountain roads take a runoff from the new-fallen snow in the lower portions of the mountains. On some highway curves the snow melts and runs across the road and dries off, but if that curve is shielded by a hillock, this result is ice by late afternoon as the sun begins to lose its punch and the shadows fall.

Also, it should be mentioned that the mountain highways are bordered by high painted stakes, six to eight feet high, as guides for the highway crew when they are using their great truck plows or blowers to clear the roads. The stakes in question were orange in color.

One late fall evening the Canter sisters were riding their Harley at very high speed as they came down the road from Lake Tahoe. They hit a patch of ice on one of the shaded turns and went over the side, dropping to the road below, or rather dropping directly above one of those orange stakes which impaled them both, the Harley proceeding on a path of self-destruction into the Truckee River far below. Not a quick or pleasant way to die it was oft said.

Their fate was a warning tale for the parents in the town and often mentioned where high-speed activities were concerned, and as a reason for denying the older youths of the area the ownership of motorcycles, however ineffective such arguments might have been for some of the independent older boys.

When the novelty of the deaths wore down, I often (boys being boys of an age) wondered whatever happened to their eagle. No one ever mentioned what happened to the bird. The Canter sisters seemed to be very fond of him. I wondered if anyone else would ever be.

Company Colors Once More

When my Dad married my mother (in Cranbrook, BC, Canada), the first thing he and my grandfather did was build a small house (shingled on the exterior as was the trend in those days). When the Great Depression crossed the border into Canada, my dad sold the place and took his bride south to Nevada where my uncle claimed there was railroad work to be had. This took my mother and father to Carlin, Nevada and to being housed (as temporarily as my dad could manage) in a converted boxcar car sitting at the side of the main SP tracks.

These were basically not much more than shelters ('as uncomfortable as you please,' my mother often remembered). I saw one of them a bit later. The interior consisted of double bunks on each side toward the rear of the car with a single chest of drawers between (and not a very large one at that). What pretended to be the kitchen had a sink with a drain which emptied to the rear side of the car onto the sandy ground below, a large, green, cold-water storage tank immediately above and an ancient, black, wood- or coal-burning stove. The tank was equipped with a pullout valve. The living room, if it could be called that, was an unfurnished area toward the front of the car. There were no windows. The only light to be had was from a couple of electric light bulbs of dim wattage (current provided by an unreliable gasoline generator down the line a little), and the open, unscreened door, of the boxcar. Necessary plumbing facilities were various ('teetering' mother's word choice again) outhouses of dubious cleanliness and maintenance.

All this came as quite a blow to my mother. She had lived as a child at Tor Castle Lodge, a building of some thirty or more rooms suitable for visits from Lord Lovat and his hunting parties, when the spirit moved them, which fronted a lovely, bubbling, rock-ridden stream which, in its turn, fed into Loch Ness.

Fortunately, we shortly moved (my sister was born in Canada) to a small yellow house in Carlin and then, anon, to Sparks (apparently for a second time, since my birth was registered in Washoe County - - 1925), and then back to the same house in Carlin.

My mother was wont to report her stunned amusement during her first encounter with the city of Sparks. You must remember, that she came from Inverness where the streets had been cobbled for over half a millennium, and gas street lights burned brightly in the night at most intersections. Her first view of the main street of Sparks ('B' Street) was of a badly graveled, dusty road replete with pecking chickens. Dad alleges she sat down in the center of the street and cried and then began to laugh.

We apparently then moved into the house on 'C' Street where I was born. And hence to another small yellow house several blocks further away, and then back to the same 'C' Street house and then, thanks to President Roosevelt and the FHA, into the house next door. That's where I spent the rest of my youth, and my dad resided until a few years after my mother died.

All the SP constructions, ranging from yard offices to company housing, were painted in two-tone. According to my father, in his more caustic moments, the colors were 'shit for brindle brown' for the trim and 'vomit yellow,' the principal color. I was never certain of the origin of the first explicative phrase, but I know a derogatory evaluation when I hear one. In his abiding contempt for company housing, if not its policies, my dad kept our house a gleaming white along with the fences forevermore.

One of the familiarities of my mother's house of origin, Tor Castle Lodge, was a splendor of fireplaces. After she left Canada, she never had one again, and was constantly asking Dad to build one for the living room. Since he and Grandpa had built such an item for the Cranbrook house, I know he was certainly capable of it. But he never quite got around to the matter. So, when I had my first regular employment at the Sprouse Reitz five and dime, I bought Mother a decorative little electric fireplace (no heat, just illusion) which resided on the top of the TV ever after. She always turned it on of an evening accompanied with a sigh of regret.

I often asked my dad about the SP's awful choice of colors. He would caustically remark that the colors, being singularly ugly and unpopular, the company probably bought them at a very low price and in enormous quantity. He was probably right. It was never difficult to determine (wherever the SP and its tracks could be found) which buildings were owned (and/or rented) by the Southern Pacific Railroad. There are telltale hearts and there are telltale colors.

The Dance Band

Wanting, for some reason or other, to be in the Sparks high school band, I took up the matter of the tenor saxophone in junior high. I came by this particular instrument because it happened to be the only one available. Maj Winters (We called him Maj, but his real name was Darrell), taught music in both the high school and the junior high, which was not all that difficult, as the schools shared the same block and were divided by tennis courts. The music room was in the high school, but it was a mere hop and a skip from the junior high (avoiding tennis balls, of course). The high school band and the high school orchestra had common members.

We took part in various parades in Reno and Sparks with the marching band which also got us free seats at all the ball games wherever they were. This meant fun trips to such towns as Elko, Ely, Carson City, Reno, Las Vegas, all those towns with high schools large enough to field an 11-man football team rather than a 6-man one. This exempted the smaller towns like Wells, Eureka and Minden. Nevada is over 110,000 square miles, and I'm sure we covered all the available highways at one time or another.

During my sophomore year, Maj decided to put together a dance band, and I happened (whatever the limits of my talent) to be the only tenor sax player available. We started out with but twelve Johnny Mercer arrangements, but frequent jobs and good fortune expanded the list considerably over the next three years. Maj often altered the arrangements based on our limited instrumentation.

Our rates were reasonable, and doubled for every hour past midnight. We usually wound up playing from about 7 p.m. to 2 a.m., so it was a profitable affair. Often I came home with $10 or more for an evening which was no small sum in the early 1940's. We also had a kitty for special requests which sometimes netted each player an additional dollar or two. This because, the longer the evening the less sober and more generous the participants, particularly in the small towns such as Verdi or Genoa.

At the beginning of my sophomore year, my worried mother decided to wait up for me. She gave it up fairly soon when I rolled in about 2:30 on several Friday and Saturday nights, tired but relatively rich. People trusted Maj Winters. He delivered those of us not yet old enough to drive, or without a car, to our own doorstep when the labor was done.

As a result of this profitable opportunity, I never learned to dance very well. We played at all the high school proms and hops and equivalent occasions. You can't be in the dance band and on the dance floor at the same time. Learning to dance on my part was long delayed.

Mr. Mercer, the arranger, assumed, as he had a right to do, a certain musical competency on the part of the musicians who would play his arrangements. He had a nasty habit in such pieces as 'Deep Purple,' 'Amapola,' 'The A Train,' and 'Marie Elena,' of leaving ten to twenty measures labeled simply, 'Solo Ad Lib.' I was merely, as Maj observed, a 'competent mechanic,' which left me at sixes and sevens about the matter of ad lib solos. Accordingly, Maj always wrote them out for me and they were paper-clipped to my music.

Our theme song, quite naturally, was 'Winter Wonderland.' Over the years we got very good at 'Winter Wonderland,' the season being irrelevant.

When I finally did learn to dance, it was in NYC. They use postage-stamp-sized dance floors which are always over-occupied. This means one does not move very much or very far. It was more a rhythmic form of the jitters than what is called dancing in the West. But it has had to do over the subsequent years.

We end on a sad note. Four of the seven band members did not return from WWII.

The Darker Side of the Force

I had many forgettable teachers. I attended their classes, performed all the proper rituals they prescribed and moved on. I cannot say what effect most of them had on me. Their names can pop up accidentally sometimes, and I can thus remember an occasional detail, but that's all.

I had a few inspiring teachers who left a major mark, and I credit them with creating in me a joy of learning, the reading habit and the gift of reasonably solid logic and perception. They come warmly to mind, from time to time, when I'm doing something of which I know they would have approved. A few other teachers stand out in my memory because they seemed hateful. They too left serious lashes on my body intellectual, and during these, my later and more introspective years, I realize they too made possible those small successes I have had in life. In fact, some of them changed my direction.

197

I have sharp memories of Mrs. Drake, a grandmother (an awesome thing to a 4th grader), who ruled her classes with a three-cornered ruler of which the palms of my hands still have a stinging recollection.

Mrs. Drake's punishment for chatter or other forms of what she construed to be misbehavior (and there were a lot of them) was to send the offender to the cloak corridor out in the hall with something long and, at the time, boring to memorize. Your daily punishment hours in the corridor ended when, and only when, you could recite, perfectly, the instrument of torture or the morning or afternoon session ended. Thus I memorized the 'Gettysburg Address,' the entire 'Constitution of the United States,' the Declaration of Independence,' the 'Rhyme of the Ancient Mariner' and many passages from the works of one William Shakespeare.

It was my unbridled hatred of, and subsequent challenge to, Mrs. Drake, which she fully recognized, that was the root of many of my cloakroom studies. I learnt much in semi-darkness and very little in the light.

Later down the line, her punishments became boons. I was frequently called upon by the American Legion and other groups to recite one or the other of the two great American documents on the 4th of July or other such occasions. It was thus I learned the value of careful articulation and the use of the hands to gather up an inattentive audience and a host of other tricks so later useful in the teaching profession. It was thus, I also won an American Legion speaking contest that provided me with my first airplane ride, to Salt Lake City from Reno, in a Ford Tri-motor equipped with wicker seats and a registered nurse as stewardess. Adventure was kindled!

She was fat. She wore a purple dress; one hoped not the same one, continually. She had a kind of acne, probably due to her diet. Her hair was always tied in a somewhat greasy bun. She had a diamond brooch she always wore. Her name was Miss Rock, but we all called her 'Miss Rock-hearted.' She taught Algebra with almost unbelievable savagery which almost always resulted in the girls in the class weeping into the chalk rail. We universally hated her.

She and I contested. My mother had taught me Algebra in the British fashion and this did not suit Miss Rock, not one little bit. The problem was that I solved the problems precisely and quickly with the right answer. Miss Rock sneered at and decried my methods. I stubbornly insisted my technique, the British approach, obviously worked as well as hers. She would rage, but I was equally stubborn. It was a year-long battle and a year-long tie.

I can still remember one exchange I had with Miss Rock when I solved an equation on the board.

'That's wrong,' she snapped.

'Is the answer wrong?' I inquired.

'No. But you've solved the problem in the wrong way.'

'How can it be wrong,' I inquired snippily, 'if I have arrived at the correct solution? How can that be wrong?'

'Take your seat and be still,' she snarled.

She'd lost, of course, and did not like it. I had won, of course, and gloried in it. We fought our way through the rest of the year, and she never managed to discomfit me at the blackboard. I got my 'A,' mutual loathing notwithstanding.

But when it came time for me to take some tests in order to enter the Navy V-5 program, which was rather more mathematically oriented than I had expected, I asked that grim woman, who, however, fierce was certainly competent, to assist me in brushing up on my Algebra, Trig and Geometry.

We set a schedule for tutoring at her house where she lived with her aging father. The house was, in my opinion, as slovenly kept as was Miss Rock. But she was, whatever else, both thorough and methodical.

When I arrived for my late afternoon or early evening tutoring, the work to be done was laid out on a large, circular dining room table, dark, un-waxed oak as I remember. We would start at one point on the circle and work our way around the table. She was grim as death, and just as demanding as always, in her lessons, and I was equally grim in my perseverance.

To my serious surprise, my much formerly assaulted algebraic methods did not come up for contest. She watched me perform, however inwardly pained she might have actually been, and when I arrived at the proper solution, merely snorted, 'satisfactory.'

I did notice one other item. Miss Rock, being very large, sweated a good deal during our working hours. But, then, so did I, as I was under considerable pressure both in matters of learning and civility.

Tutored for something over four months, I took the required Navy tests and passed them handily.

The Ends of Childhood

No! I don't mean the end of childhood, I mean the ends of childhood, and the one certainty of which I can assure you, circa the early 1930's, is that the ends of the childhood I knew were not adulthood.

The sad truth of it, these days, is that today's children are not permitted a childhood. If they are, it is directed, governed, disciplined, monitored, paved and pointed into a future which, when one is nine or ten, is inconceivably distant on the horizon.

Accordingly, one is in an adult-oriented prison of long, thin corridors, the ends of which are invisible and the purposes of which are puzzling.

I knew, as most of my friends knew, that our parents, being foreigners, were different than some mysterious group called 'the average American family.' My mother spoke English with a Scottish accent, my father with a Canadian one. As my father often remarked, 'Americans sound as though they are talking through a tin can.' My mother was duly horrified at the awful examples of improper English she heard over the radio and in the markets.

The parents of some of my pals did not speak English. Mrs. Barbieri spoke only Italian, though I can recall no problem in communicating with her when invited to join Reno and Mario for dinner. Bill Zenclusen's parents spoke German at home and Bill did the translating. We seemed to have no difficulty. It was a little trickier dealing with Honroko Ishii's mother as there's a mighty distance between the Orient and the Occident not only in language, but in custom. But Dr. Ishii spoke excellent English, learned, as he would point out, in medical school. Chewy Gonzales's (We were embarrassed to use his correct first name, Jesus.) dad spoke some English, Mrs. Gonzales nothing worth noting. Dean McNeilly's parents were more difficult. They happened to be both deaf and dumb and spoke only in sign language and special grunts which Dean and/or his brother could readily interpret. It was the silence in the house that was awesome to say nothing of flashing fingers and other signs. The food, though, was excellent.

I was, by any measure, the smallest, fairest-skinned and blondest of any of our group. My tongue was my instrument of defense and control. Perhaps, more influential was that my mother, truly multi-lingual and well-educated, could speak to any of my buddies in the language they were accustomed to hear at home. Likewise, she could chat with their parents handily on the telephone.

The folk in question found my mother's slight Scottish accent reflected in her linguistic conversations with them. I never noticed any accent, either my own pre-school Scottish burr, or my father's broader Canadian sound. They appeared, as though by magic, only when I had been away during WWII and returned much later.

We also had to be very, very careful. My mother's ears were tuned to oaths in all the languages concerned and reprimands were swift, verbal and re-enforced with a waving, fly swatter which she was not hesitant to use on any vulgar child within her immediate range. Parental anger over discipline from other parents would have been laughed off the planet at the time.

I cannot remember the Depression years as all that grim, though now I know it left many adults scarred and battered. We knew nothing of this. We were busy building, along the shores of the Truckee River, a raft so we could float along like Huckleberry Finn. I had read the book and loved explaining it to Chewy, Honroko, or Mario who had not read it and showed no inclination to do so. Our raft was made of water-soaked logs. It is fortunate we never finished, even over several summers, and hence never launched, as it would no doubt have immediately sunk to the bottom of the Truckee.

As I have mentioned before, I had a heavy English tome called, 'A Boy's Own Papers,' replete with great stories and all manner of things to build. It was this gift of special knowledge of new games and new devices that marked me as the spokesman of and the leader of our gang. We were a gang, no doubt, but not of the type the police have to deal with these days.

We played war with rubber guns or snowballs. We built forts and other defensive bastions. We had secret huts and tunnels and tree houses. We sometimes viewed the adult world eye-to-eye because of the stilts we made. We were always surrounded by barks of many happy dogs. We built and flew homemade kites with knotted sections of string, and rag tails, and prayed for heavy March winds, and had wonderful kite fights high in the cloudless Nevada skies. The trick was to cross the other fellow's kite from above, feed a sudden spurt of string, and have your kite's rag tail drop on his kite and send it spinning out of control. If he did not have the skill to recover, the kite crashed, we tracked it down and helped him rebuild it with newspapers, hand-carved sticks and paste made from flour.

We dug trenches in empty lots in the neighborhood and then roofed them with willow branches, and dug a fireplace in the back of a trench and made a vertical hole for a chimney. We would build fires in our 'huts' and roast marshmallows or hot dogs, or potatoes, or whatever else could be cooked on a willow spit.

By hook (or maybe by crook) we always managed to filch some potatoes out of somebody's garden, or con grocers Semenza or Hanson into giving us a couple of hot dogs to be sliced with jack-knives and spitted. We tried roasting carrots once. Ugh!

School was three seasons of torture between one-season of freedom and glory. Lessons came easily to me, so I often helped the others with their homework. My writing was fluent (Shakespeare and Dickens were often read at our house), so I ghost-dictated an endless sea of themes and papers, and solved an enormous number of other's math problems. I learned to lecture, and they learned to listen about American and World History. Though I did not know it, I had already found my future profession.

When I entered high school one Bovee Dodds was on the top of the honor roll with a 1.1 average. (1.0 was an A, 1.5 A- and so on down.) I knocked him off with a straight 1.0 the first semester and held that position through graduation. Hence, it was assumed I was a bookworm and would not be interested in parties or other frivolities. Only the members of the original grammar-school gang knew better, and may many blessings rest eternally on their several houses.

I became, as I wanted, the editor of the 'Streamliner,' the high school paper. I became, as my mother insisted, the valedictorian. I managed to do all my homework in study halls and hence never brought any work home. I kept mother at bay with the simple statement that if I failed to get a 1.0 average anytime along the line, I would resort to homework. I never had to.

Childhood came to an abrupt halt upon entrance to high school. Or so we thought. Youth ended equally abruptly at high school graduation as we joined the Navy, the Marines, or the Army to serve in WWII.

Though they did not know it, half the males in my senior class had no future. The rest of us had no planned future, but I think we managed rather well, and part of that management came from the fact that we did have an unstructured and self-adaptive childhood.

The Flume

The particular flume in question was somewhat to the West of Reno. We would ride our bikes the ten miles or so to get to it. Our flume was a wooden ditch raised on a high trestle. Its purpose was to ultimately feed water into the power company's generators. The flume was an old one, its sides coated in wonderful slippery green slime. Every six feet along the top a wooden two-by-four held the ditch together. The sides leaked a bit, making for green growth underneath. But our purpose for the flume was excitement and joy riding.

We would go near the top of the hill whence the flume appeared, climb the trestle, and then, hanging on one of the two-by-fours, lower ourselves into the rushing stream in such a way we would be riding on our backs, feet first, in the direction of the power station. We always guessed the water was going forty-miles-an-hour, but we really did not know. It was a glorious fast ride with a potential hazard at the end.

The flume ended in the open air and sent a great roaring stream of water downward into a sloping net (to keep debris (and quite possibly small boys) out of the concrete tunnel which then led to the turbine blades below. It was said that if you were hurled against the steel mesh net, you had just a few seconds to climb rapidly to get out of the awful water pressure that would either crush or drown you. And how did we avoid this fate?

Near the dangerous end of the flume we had nailed three white flags on the crossing two-by-fours and, last of all, one red flag, indicating, if you missed catching it, you were going to be hurled into space and against the net and life, as we thought we knew it, might possibly end.

It was rumored that one fellow the guys did not like never grabbed the three white or the red-marked two-by-four because they had taken the flags down to get even with him. He was allegedly hurled against the net, which broke, and was launched into the concrete tunnel and turned into hamburger by the turbine blades. The story continued with the grim addition that people in Reno and Sparks were stunned when they turned on their taps one afternoon and the water ran red. This I knew was not possible unless the entire Truckee River was capable of turning red from the input of the excess water from the power company. When I grew older, I checked around, but no adult had ever heard the tale and the power company had no records of such a tragedy.

I always managed to catch the first white-flagged two-by-four. I was never that much the risk taker. Some of the braver fellows liked to wait until the last minute and catch the red marked crosspiece. They probably joined the parachute troops in WWII, or the Navy Seals.

We used the OED's definition in reverse. For us, 'to go *down* the flume' meant to take a great risk or to die. When one of my gang had died of polio we said, 'He went down the flume and missed the red flag.' That was our way of contending with the grim reaper in a time when he made fairly frequently calls (polio, diphtheria, influenza, scarlet fever, and pneumonia to name just a few). For the survivors life, while always hazardous, seemed all the more delicious.

Some children were sometimes quarantined. We were forbidden to play with them. During a polio wave, we were not allowed to go to the movies or the library, and sometimes the schools closed their doors for a while. Death, it seemed, was never distant, not even for the young, though this was seldom discussed. We heard our parents talking to other parents about 'poor little Billy Smith or the late Mary Jane,' But we were never made privy to the grimmer details.

We were constantly advised by our mother's that we might put an eye out (those rubber guns), or break our necks (tree climbing), or come down with a chill (playing in puddles in those rare Nevada rains), or blow off a hand and bleed to death (fire crackers), or be blinded (rubber guns and fire crackers again) or catch a dread and fatal disease, if we did not wash our hands before eating). We did not always heed these warnings and survived anyway, and never forgot to count ourselves lucky.

The Ice Man

I can recall when we gave up the cooler that lowered into the ground below the pantry and 'modernized' with an ice box. This brought the Union Ice man to our home about once a week. My mother would put a green card in the living room window that showed whether she wanted 25, 50, 75 or 100 lbs. of ice. The Union Ice man wore a leather apron, not across his middle, but rather down his back. He had great ice tongs and would seize the 100 lb. cake of ice (which we ordered as often as we could afford it), hurl it over his back and haul it straight through the front porch, the living room, and into the kitchen and deposit it in the upper left-hand corner of the ice box. There was a drip pan under the ice box and it was my task to get on my knees, lift the panel and check the pan from time to time and empty it if it was full. Later, Dad simply bored a hole through the floor and extended the drip tube down under the house. In the desert country with dry sand below, this presented no moisture problem, even in the winter. I was relieved of a chore thanks to his ingenuity. One chore gone — but there were plenty of others.

Service people these days don't quite have the courtesy or thoughtfulness of those of yesteryear. The Union Ice man was well aware that neighborhood children loved to filch little chunks of ice from the truck for sipping purposes. In our neighborhood, he always chipped some nifty chunks and left them handy when he was inside putting the ice away. He, knowing that those of us with skates, when the street was finally paved, loved to hang on to the back of the truck for a free ride for a block or so, always drove very carefully and quite slowly. We thought we were terribly sneaky and clever. He probably had children of his own.

I also remember the milkman would, if his bills were promptly paid (and we always managed that somehow), leave a-once-a-week bonus — a small half-pint of rich whipping cream — a monumental luxury to steady customers. Mother would send me to the backyard to pick strawberries (during the season) or to the grocery store for fresh peaches. Strawberries and cream! Peaches and cream! It was an event to be cherished in memory. In the winter, she would buy a pie from Mr. Thorson and whip the cream for topping. Or, failing that, we had the luxury of rich cream on our oatmeal.

Only Mr. Lightfoot, who worked for the Sierra Pacific Power Company, had a job steady enough to afford a refrigerator. I was a fascinating mechanism — a white, square box on legs, made by General Electric. On top perched a round coil, not too different from the shape of some of our modern air conditioners. This was a miracle machine. It not only made ice cubes, though not very many, but kept ice cream frozen — a wonderful thing.

In my family's case, whenever we decided to have ice cream, I had to mount my bicycle immediately after the main course and pedal rapidly to Ramos Drug store. I would buy a pint of whatever flavored ice cream we wished and then head home lickety split. The only advantage was we had to eat the entire pint or, on rare occasion, quart, at one sitting or it would melt away. My Dad finally bought a refrigerator, a 'Coldspot,' shortly after the end of WWII, but I was never home again to take advantage of it.

Another of my bicycle duties included pedaling over to the Zenclusen farm to buy a carton or two of eggs. Eggs were twelve cents a dozen and my mother preferred them fresh.

Sometimes, I could take a small wooden tub with me (about a quart in size I would estimate) and Mrs. Zenclusen would fill it with freshly churned butter. That was a bit more expensive, as I recall — something on the order of a quarter. Mother thought it was worth it.

Later a strange kind of butter substitute arrived. It came in a plastic bag and was white. It was called oleomargarine or something equally complicated. It was forbidden that the margarine arrive in a butter color or cubes, a dairy interest lobby's victory. Inside the plastic bag was a small capsule of coloring. One of my chores was to squeeze the contents of the bag back and forth until such time as I had achieved a uniform butter color throughout.

It would then be spooned into a shallow metal tray which Mother would set on top of the ice in the icebox. I always suggested we just leave the stuff white, but she was convinced the color enhanced the flavor. Somewhere along the line she gave up butter entirely because it was too expensive and too, milk had risen to six or seven cents a quart — truly outrageous.

War Inconvenience

If I'm counting right, I had just been 15 years old for 17 days when the Japanese Empire attacked the United States at Pearl Harbor and other places on December 7, 1941. At the time I was working (before and after school hours and all other days, including eight hours Sunday for stocking shelves) for the Sprouse-Reitz five and dime store in downtown Sparks. The store was managed by my first regular (and ever wonderfully generous and kind) employer, Bryan Laviega.

Shortly after Pearl Harbor we received orders to destroy all Japanese merchandise carried in the five and dime. There were a considerable number of items ranging from a variety of earthenware teapots to tiny little paper parasols to dispose of. My job was to clear all those bins in the store divided from one another by glass strips and store the Japanese merchandise in the stock room. American replacements, we were assured, would soon follow. They never did.

Mr. Laviega pondered the problem for a good while and decided it would be fun to package various items and give them to people in town as surprise gifts. We prepared an enormous box of such merchandise to be sent to the Sparks High shop teacher, 'Wink' Hastings, a friend of Mr. Laviega's. He had many other friends, so I was busy packing merchandise for some weeks and seeing to its transport to various people via the use of the Hanson grocery store delivery boy and his pickup truck. He was 17 and had a license. We had a lot of fun making our surprise deliveries.

We were supposed to declare that the merchandise in question had been shipped to the recipient by the friendly Emperor of Japan. We were instructed to deliver the goods, bow, and say 'Ah so,' as we departed. This we did accompanied by a lot of giggling.

I was given permission to take home any amount of the various items that might be useful. Amongst other things I remember presenting my mother with twelve different-sized earthenware teapots (very British in the matter of tea she was). There were a host of other little kitchen gimmicks, decorative statuary, etc. that I brought home, including a lot of interesting little boxes which could only be opened by sliding secret panels this way and that. I also remember some decorated Japanese tea sets (pots, cups, saucers et al) that my mother highly prized and often used for show when visiting gossips came our way.

During the first week's aftermath of Pearl Harbor, a number of the women in the neighborhood consulted my mother about whether or not to flee to the Midwest. Mother was consulted because she had worked in London, England, during WWI when the Germans were doing a bit of spotty bombing of the city, very shocking in its day, almost comparable to the bombing of Nanking later in the thirties by the Japanese.

Mother, as usual, had me boil water, heat the pot, and make tea for her lady friends. This it seems, is what the British do when a crisis arrives. It settles the nerves and makes time for an intelligent analysis of the situation.

Mother advised her fearful lady friends that any bombing by the Japanese would likely be confined to our major cities, but since she had been there and knew the distances involved rather well, she thought it to be highly unlikely. But, she opined, should the Japanese invade the West Coast, as imagined, there was the matter of the High Sierras to deal with and, quite frankly, she did not think the Japanese were, with such extended supply lines, up to that sort of misadventure. She did dismiss rather sharply the idea that America would beat the Japanese in six weeks or less.

She did remind them that, as she watched trucks of scrap iron pass our street on the way to San

Francisco to be shipped to Japan over the years, she had frequently said, 'You'll be getting it back sooner than you think!' Mother was, on that occasion, just the one to rub it in! Her son, I regret to say, inherited a good bit of that same tendency.

I don't recall much about the other varied items I brought home from the Sprouse-Reitz store, but I can attest that some of the earthenware teapots were still in use in our house when I went off to war (July 1943 at the age of 17) and were still happily in use when I returned (September 15, 1945). Mother was not given to trivial prejudices.

Epilogue

I have had the enormous good fortune during my childhood of living in a world of contrasts. Both my parents came from other lands and had views and habits somewhat alien to the 'American way.'

My mother was a well-educated woman who spoke and read several languages fluently. My father was not well educated, but clever and hard working. Their utterly different views, because I loved them both, taught me tolerance and a certain willingness to ponder the ways of people who did not think in my particular and peculiar fashion. I count that a blessing.

I also learned to dismiss anyone who, over the age of 17, wished to saddle his parents with his personal flaws or misadventures. On discovery that my parents were 'different' and that I was therefore somehow out of tune with my native land here and there, I took a hard look in the mirror and told myself my troubles from that point on were of my own making, and so they have been.

My dad, in a moment of rare philosophy once said, 'You know, I was born before the air plane and I have lived to see men land on the moon. That's one helluva lot of change.'

A misfortune from my own point of view, now that I am 82 and, as it is said, have one foot on a banana peel and the other in the grave, is that my own parents were far too busy surviving to tell me many tales of their own childhoods. I would love, in my later years, to have known them.

So, for my daughters and grandchildren, I have produced this small work. Too, my friends tell me it is not so much what I have written about my childhood and youth that attracts them but the different memories my memories trigger in them.

That, it seems to me, is sufficient reward.

Printed in the United States
90347LV00001B/7-33/A